T0338123

DREAMWORLDS of ALABAMA

PELHAM, "THE GREAT CANNONEER"

DREAMWORLDS
of
ALABAMA

Allen Shelton

University of Minnesota Press

MINNEAPOLIS

LONDON

The publication of this book was assisted by a bequest from Josiah H. Chase to honor his parents, Ellen Rankin Chase and Josiah Hook Chase, Minnesota territorial pioneers.

Copyright 2007 by the Regents of the University of Minnesota

All rights reserved. No part of this publication may be reproduced, stored in a retrieval system, or transmitted, in any form or by any means, electronic, mechanical, photocopying, recording, or otherwise, without the prior written permission of the publisher.

Published by the University of Minnesota Press
111 Third Avenue South, Suite 290
Minneapolis, MN 55401-2520
http://www.upress.umn.edu

Library of Congress Cataloging-in-Publication Data
Shelton, Allen (Allen C.)
Dreamworlds of Alabama / Allen Shelton.
   p.   cm.
Includes bibliographical references.
ISBN: 978-0-8166-5034-7   ISBN-10: 0-8166-5034-9 (hc : alk. paper)
ISBN: 978-0-8166-5035-4   ISBN-10: 0-8166-5035-7 (pb : alk. paper)
1. Jacksonville (Ala.)—Biography. 2. Jacksonville (Ala.)—Social life and customs. 3. Farm life—Alabama—Jacksonville. 4. Shelton, Allen (Allen C.)—Childhood and youth. 5. Shelton, Allen (Allen C.)—Family. 6. Pelham, John, 1838–1863—Influence. 7. Benjamin, Walter, 1892–1940—Influence. 8. Hubbard, Elizabeth, d. 1938—Influence. 9. Alabama—History—Miscellanea. 10. Teachers—New York (State)—Buffalo—Biography. I. Title.
F334.J33S54 2007
976.1'63—dc22   2007021253

Printed in the United States of America on acid-free paper
The University of Minnesota is an equal-opportunity educator and employer.

25 24 23 22 21 20 19 18   10 9 8 7 6 5 4 3 2

For Tyree Shelton

and those I loved

AC, Mary, Mary Janie, and Pearl

in the world I lost to write this book

Contents

Acknowledgments

My mother's father was a professor of education at a small teachers' college in my hometown. He died within months after I was born, but he left me his library to grow up in, an environment that I've never left. His father was a schoolteacher in a remote rural county in Alabama. My mother taught school off and on her whole life. For this disposition I'm not altogether thankful. After leaving my farm, I spent nearly a decade on the road as a migrant professor crisscrossing the country. Because of this, the book was written in successive stages in Buffalo out of materials taken from different moments in my past and auditioned in front of students across the country. I owe my devoted students a debt of gratitude for helping me work out the telling of these accounts. "The Mark on the Spade" was completed in 2002 from materials I'd been working on since 1994. "Planchette, My Love" took another two years, working with even older materials. Without the support of Raphael Allen, Howard Becker, Susan Buck-Morss, Norman Denzin, Danielle Egan, Gary Alan Fine, Debra Heisler, Stephen Pfohl, Jake and Jackie Shelton, Eleni Stecopoulos, Jonathon Welch and Talking Leaves . . . Books, Paul Willis, Jonathan Wynn, and Arthur Wilke, these essays could not have been written. I owe more than I can say to these individuals. The last essays were produced in 2005 and 2006 with the additional support of my editor at the University of Minnesota Press, Richard Morrison, Kathy Psomiades' astute reading, Paul Bugyi, Henry Sussman, Derek Sayer, Anne Costello's careful editing, Yoke-Sum Wong, and Kathleen Stewart. Their guidance and care were indispensable. I owe much to Terri Dayan and a special debt to Molly Jarboe, who was caught nearest me in the inner circle of producing this book.

Inside my grandmother's hope chest, I found a photograph from the late nineteenth century of my grandfather's mother as a young woman. She is sitting outside on a porch in a high-backed chair with a black curtain draped across the clapboard siding framing her. Her hair is up, and she is wearing a long-sleeved dress with a white band around her neck. She is facing the viewer with her eyes wide open and her left arm propped on top of an enormous book. While my mother looked for angels in the netherworld, I found mine in my own history; she is for me what Walter Benjamin's angel was for him, a sign of an apocalypse. She oversaw my long trips across the country and my struggles to write. Underneath her gaze the martyrdoms of Joan of Arc, John Pelham, and Patrick Keim burst into the flames that opened up a world for me.

Preface
You Are Worth Many Sparrows

In 1863 in an indecisive skirmish at Kelly's Ford, Major John Pelham was hit with a shell fragment in the head. Presumed to be dead on the battlefield, Pelham was thrown across the back of a horse. Only later was he discovered to be still alive, but by then it was too late. He died four days later. On the day of his fatal wounding he was enjoying the company of Virginia ladies when he heard the gunfire and rushed to the battle line. He was a valiant man.[1] He was twenty-six years old, still boyish and extremely handsome. At the news of his death, the Confederate commander J. E. B. Stuart was moved to say:

> The major-general commanding approaches with reluctance the painful duty of announcing to the division its irreparable loss in the death of Major John Pelham, commanding the Horse Artillery. He fell mortally wounded in the battle of Kellysville, March 17 with the battle cry on his lips, and the light of victory beaming from his eye. . . . His eye had glanced on every battlefield of this army from the First Manassas to the moment of his death, and he was, with a single exception, a brilliant actor in them all. The memory of "the gallant Pelham," his manly virtues, his noble nature and purity of character, are enshrined as a sacred legacy in the hearts of all who knew him. His record has been bright and spotless, his career brilliant and successful.[2]

His coffin was covered with wisteria cuttings left by female admirers in Richmond and shipped south by rail to Jacksonville, Alabama. His death had no effect on the outcome of the war, despite General Lee reportedly saying that "if he had had a hundred men like Pelham the war would soon be over." The war was over by the spring of 1865 without him. John Pelham was a man bred to be killed. But his death and his remembrance changed the landscape around my childhood. From the cuttings on his coffin, wisteria first came to the small town of Jacksonville. Around the boyish figure of John Pelham, a thick skeletal prosthetic of vines and blooms burst into the northeastern Alabama woods, sharing space with the hickories and lilacs and catbrier. The effect was to start the creation of an entirely new dreamworld of Alabama, unimaginable if John Pelham had lived. His death baptized the landscape.

John Pelham's contribution as a living man was his astute use of horse-drawn artillery. At the Battle of Fredericksburg, using a single twelve-pounder Napoleon cannon, Pelham harassed the advancing Union Army so effectively that five Union batteries began responding to what they thought was a full Confederate battery. Dead, he was as a doorway between this world and the supernatural. I would see him whenever I accompanied my grandmother to the cemetery to tend the grave of her husband, Eli Landers. Pelham grew up on a plantation near Cane Creek, five miles west of where I lived in Jacksonville. He was undistinguished as a boy. He attended West Point, and when the war erupted, he was commissioned as a first lieutenant in the Army of the Confederacy. He formed and led a six-gun battery that was recognized for its discipline and drill-like precision in battle. Here Pelham found himself. In the end, his greatest achievement was not in battle but in his attributed introduction of wisteria into northeast Alabama. Pelham changed the shape of haunting in Jacksonville. The purple clusters of blooms entered the local botanical mythology, along with the Christlike dogwood and the red buds of the Judas tree. John Pelham would step up alongside Jesus in this Protestant world to command the dead. He taught me the first lessons of my life.

One of John Pelham's descendants, or at least she claimed to be in her public appearances at women's club meetings in Jacksonville, was Elizabeth Hubbard. She was the wife of a Birmingham steel executive who had amassed an enormous fortune in the aftermath of the Spanish-American War. Privately, she went even further. She claimed to be the reincarnation of Major John Pelham and would point to his photograph and her own likeness to it, recounting vivid descriptions of her death in Virginia. As a young woman she was a student of the psychologist G. Stanley Hall at Clark University in Worcester, Massachusetts. Elizabeth Hubbard attended all five of Sigmund Freud's lectures in a gymnasium in 1909. It was standing room only. "Meeting Freud was," she would later write in her diary, "the decisive moment in my life." Freud was paid $714.60 to give the lectures. Elizabeth Hubbard came back to Alabama, married, and became an advocate of mental health reform. She toured the state giving talks to faculty wives' clubs, garden clubs, and meetings of the Daughters of the American Revolution and the Daughters of the Confederacy. She believed that memorials to the Confederate dead and dogwoods spreading under oaks would act as a gentle skeletal framework for the sick and the well alike, holding them like mothers. Instead of shock and insulin treatments inside a network of cells, Elizabeth Hubbard envisioned gardens, sitting vistas, and streets overlooked by memorials and trees where the dead, mockingbirds, butterflies, and families would interact on the same plane. What was remarkable is how closely she approximated an image in Freud's 1929 work *Civilization and Its Discontents* in which the city of Rome acted as a metaphor for the mind. However, where Freud saw a city emptied of all living things as a model for the mind, she saw a living exoskeleton, an ecosystem in which ghosts posed in marble in a floral underworld.

In 1905 an Italian marble statue of John Pelham was erected at the entrance of the Jacksonville City Cemetery. John Pelham was finally mineralized. He was portrayed like a praying mantis on a leaf, perfectly still, folded like a saint in prayer, the carnivorousness of the sword suspended from a wide sash, asleep. Behind him in ordered rows of simple crosses were hundreds of Confederate dead. Thirty percent of the enlisted men from this small town were killed in the war. Thirty-three years later, Elizabeth Hubbard too was dead. She died, like my mother, of a massive brain aneurysm. Those who believed in her story about Pelham pointed out he died of a head wound as well. Shortly before her death, she wrote in her diary a barely legible note in soft pencil at the bottom of the page, "planchette, my love." She was buried on a hillside delicately covered with trees and statues outside of Birmingham, overlooking Highway 78 as it runs east to Atlanta and west to Tuscaloosa. The Freedom Riders would have passed her grave on their way to New Orleans in the 1960s. It was the only thing on that stretch of highway to look at.

Despite her work, the city of Jacksonville didn't develop entirely in line with Elizabeth Hubbard's vision and hints of money. The city had its own momentum. The main street was named Pelham Road. The elm trees were killed in the blight. There were plaques and two statues. John Pelham stood over the city cemetery at the edge of town and what was called Needmore, the black part of town. A good half mile away was the statue of a Confederate soldier in the middle of the town square surrounded by evergreen trees and machine guns from World War I. Informally, there were the antebellum houses and their Victorian cousins slowly disintegrating as the money moved out toward the newer parts of town. Instead of butterflies, large black grasshoppers took over the rambling gardens. The addition of mechanized weaponry was not part of Hubbard's vision. Nor was the disintegration of Reconstruction race relations. The name Needmore vanished. Her vision was another version of a floral dead zone, a deserted memory palace, with only the slenderest possibility that her nostalgia might turn inside out into a different kind of dreamworld.

For the German critic Walter Benjamin, whose life overlapped with Elizabeth Hubbard's, a dreamworld was the phantasmagoria that sprang up in the shopping arcades of the nineteenth century where dream fetishes and commodity fetishes were so intertwined as to be indistinguishable.[3] The effect was bedazzlement in the face of a new kind of heavenly city or an intensely luxuriant ecosystem with strange new creatures like combs that swam in aquarium-like display cases, corsets that stood like statues among stacks of pressed cotton shirts, air rifles named for the goddess of the hunt, and faces on billboards that steadily grew into gigantic smiles. Mythic creatures populated the ur-forest of the modern city. Benjamin's dreamworld was a hybrid space made from dreams, commodities, and memory compressed together under pressure. The dreamworld was the luxuriant space that developed alongside the arid worlds Marx describes in *Capital*. Compared to Elizabeth Hubbard's world, Benjamin's is

less arabesque and more enthralled by the new ecosystem of magical commodities flourishing in the arcade's beds and undergrowth.
But in Benjamin's public writings there are no animals, no vines or
personal grief and scars that can mar the page. Hubbard wasn't as
enamored by the shine on things for the new world as Benjamin
was. Out of Elizabeth Hubbard's obsession with Pelham something
terrible, beautiful, and at times humane developed from the scars
and pains that can be felt in her diary. She never divulged her own
psychoanalytic material directly, preferring, like Walter Benjamin,
to write in an allegorical style about her personal grief. But what if
Benjamin's and Hubbard's landscapes were overlaid like transpar-
ent maps on the same terrain? *Dreamworlds of Alabama* is another
name for the mysteries of capital reaching into memory and the ecosystem around John Pelham.

I was born in this dreamworld. I grew up in Jacksonville and
around Rabbittown. My son is named Tyree Landers Shelton, and
his namesake was a soldier in the American Revolution. The soldier
is buried in a small churchyard seventeen miles from where Tyree
was born. I worked on a cattle farm for twenty-one years, building
barbed wire fences, herding cows on foot with a four-foot hickory
stick, delivering breech-birthed calves, inoculating, tattooing, and
hauling hay. I still have my fence tool with me. My other tools have
been stolen or interred in long-term storage in a shed back in Alabama. My fence tool looks like a prehistoric bird of prey. It has a
sharp, slightly curved beak on one side and a flat hammerhead on
the other. It resembles a pair of pliers that has undergone a radical mutation in black steel with grappling teeth in the center and
flat molars on both sides. The fence tool is a formidable creature,
though it weighs only two pounds. It lies on top of my books now

like Cerberus. Despite the evidence, acquaintances look at the fence tool as something I picked up at a yard sale. Inevitably, they make a disparaging comment, such as "Did you work in a Hugo Boss suit?" "There is no Hugo Boss," I respond. "It's a design without a designer, a corporate fiction without a single author." I speak in what others often hear as a strange accent. My past can't be located. I live in Buffalo, New York, an exile from the South. But these aren't Yankee dreams, even though my past seems like a fabrication, a dreamworld in which I'm a paper character and not a historical participant with scars from barbed wire ripping under the pressure and flying through the air like a swarm of bees, or a horse rearing up and banging its head into mine, exploding my forehead. Yellow jackets were drawn to the blood as I sat on a stump holding my head like I was praying over the puddle of blood. I remember this even though it might be classified as ethnographic fiction. The deepest scars can't be seen on my skin. Every day I miss the dreamworld I grew up in. This book is about how I lost this world. In each essay I wrote, I lost a little more of what I had already lost. That is another cost of reclamation from a faraway place.

A decisive part of Walter Benjamin's career was the denial of his dissertation by his committee. His dissertation was unreadable according to one of his professors. The work was later published and favorably reviewed, but no matter. Benjamin was a Jew, and the worsening political situation in Germany would have eventually forced him out. But the premature expulsion forced him into a more and more precarious financial and emotional situation. His circuitous exile became a feature of his work, informing not only his memory pieces about his childhood in Berlin, his affinity for Proust and Kafka, but also the concepts and methods he utilized.

In his essay "A Berlin Chronicle," Benjamin writes pleasantly about being a stranger in a strange land:

> But to lose oneself in a city—as one loses oneself in a forest—this calls for quite a different schooling. Then, signboards and street names, passers-by, roofs, kiosks, and bars must speak to the wanderer like a snapping twig under his feet in the forest, like the startling call of the bittern in the distance, like the sudden stillness of a clearing with a lily standing erect at its center. Paris taught me this art of straying; it fulfilled a dream that had shown its first traces in the labyrinths on the blotting pages of my school exercise books. Nor is it to be denied that I penetrated to its innermost place, the Minotaur's chamber, the only difference being that this mythological monster had three heads: those of the occupants of the small brothel on rue de la Harpe, in which, summoning my last reserves of strength (and not entirely without an Adriana's thread), I set my foot. But if Paris thus answered my most uneasy expectations, from another side it surpassed my graphic fantasies. The city, as it disclosed itself to me in the footsteps of the hermetic tradition that I can trace back at least as far as Rilke, whose guardian at that time was Franz Hessel, was a maze not only of paths but also of tunnels. I cannot think of the underworld of the Metro and the North–South line opening their hundreds of shafts all over the city, without recalling my endless flaneries.[4]

Set against the backdrop of Benjamin's forced migratory wanderings, the lines twist in a kind of anguish. Disasters seemed to be Benjamin's fate. He worked steadily at fulfilling his exile. He suspected his committee's reactions and apparently helped to push them to their decision with his own acts. His parents, sensing that their son would end up as a writer, gave him a secret Gentile name to publish under, according to his childhood friend. Benjamin rejected it. Benjamin, in a passage from his only other published book, *One-Way Street*, writes his own ending:

> The bourgeois interior of the 1860s to the 1890s—with its gigantic sideboards distended with carvings, the sunless corners where potted palms sit, the balcony embattled behind its balustrade, and the long corridors with their singing gas flames—fittingly houses only the corpse. "On this sofa the aunt cannot but be murdered." The soulless luxuriance of the furnishing becomes true comfort only in the presence of a dead body. Far more interesting than the Oriental landscapes in detective novels, is that rank Oriental inhabiting their interiors: the Persian carpet and the ottoman, the hanging lamp and the genuine dagger from Caucasia. Behind the heavy, gathered Kilian tapestries, the master of the house has orgies with his share certificates, feels himself the Eastern merchant, the indolent pasha in the caravanserai of otiose enchantment, until that dagger in its silver sling above the divan puts an end, one fine afternoon, to his siesta and himself. This character of the bourgeois apartment, tremulously awaiting the nameless murderer like a lascivious old lady her gallant . . .[5]

It seems Benjamin was slowly lowering himself into a box of crowded sentences. He was burying himself alive in a scriptural shell designed by himself in which the murderer has his own face, like a Minotaur's, grafted onto another's body coming for him. Pelham's death was no different. He wasn't ordered to the line. He was drawn by something else inside him to join the cavalry charge, to find the chance explosion near his head and the configuration of circumstances that would kill him. The dreamworld inside Pelham was lined up with the shift in tactics and the mechanization of battle in the Civil War to come spilling out. But what shape it would take was unclear. Pelham was ambivalent about secession, as was the whole state. The vote to secede was decided by only two thousand votes. A county in the north of Alabama seceded from the Confederacy. It was in his remembrance that the doomed Southern knight fully emerged as a dream figure in the public landscape. Pelham was a more muscular embodiment of the Southern Gothic, as if he and his gun battery somehow slipped out into Jacksonville through a landscape created by Edgar Allan Poe. How exactly I became infected with this world escapes me. My best guess is an architectural virus that my mother and grandmother imparted to me. On the day I hung up my nail apron and propped my posthole digger against the shed wall and stepped into college as an adjunct professor, I was ready to be John Pelham. And that moment came soon enough. The department, in an effort to raise money from alumni, was putting together a newsletter. This memo was in my mailbox:

> Hey there colleagues!! Well no more Ms. Nice!! Need your information ASAP for the department newsletter: about you, about your work/projects, new things to accomplish, recipes, jokes, tidbits, your predictions/revelation to the future, etc.—various important and earthshaking stuff like that. . . . (Or—second option, I CAN make it all up!)

The author was a second-year assistant professor. She was thirty-eight years old; short, stocky, and lived with her cat in a small apartment. She had red hair and freckles. Her hair was cut in a thick pageboy crop just beneath her ears. She wore blue jeans and boots with high heels. On her office walls were framed photographs of Captain Kirk, Cher, and Chuck Norris. She described herself as a feminist. At Christmas, she and her cat sent out cards. She signed for both of them. Her closest friend was another second-year faculty member. She had a crush on him and his wife had a crush on her. He was a popular teacher. She was unpopular. He would get tenure early. She would be denied. It was a tight circle. But these events were still years away. She couldn't guess that she would lose or that her memo would do me in. She wished it. She just couldn't see it. What I wrote in my biography helped set a series of events into motion that are still pushing me around. I would get ensnared in a major football scandal that rocked the school and ended with me getting death threats. I was blamed for organizing the first civil rights protest in the school's history over an Old South Parade. And I was there at the beginning of the grade scandal involving hundreds if not thousands of students that took fifteen years to come to the surface in the *New York Times*. I lost each encounter. The sketch I produced captured me at the moment just before becoming a migrant academic. Within a year, I would be on the road out of the South and my home. When I read the sketch now, it's like looking at a photograph of Billy the Kid before his first shooting. What I wrote makes the cracks and fissures in my own life seeable as a recipe for what I would do. There are indications that bad things are about to happen.

Allen Shelton, instructor. I am writing this short note, not with a word processor, but with my new Waterman fountain pen. No doubt this pen is almost identical to the one Claude Levi-Strauss finds in the hand of a Native American in full regalia, sitting in the New York Public Library in the early 1940s, taking notes from an anthropology text on Native American traditions. I have bought a fountain pen, forking out sixty American dollars in hopes that I can approximate what it is I find so mysterious about this image. I have started to think about writing about my own Native American past. My grandfather was one-quarter Choctaw. Running through all of this is the salesman's line, "it will last a lifetime," and a comment a devoted fountain pen user drops, "it takes on the shape and angle of your hand forever."

It's not hard to see the problems. The passage starts with one—Allen Shelton, instructor, not assistant professor. I was ABD (all but dissertation). I was paid $21,000 a year to teach twelve courses. I was hired on a year-to-year basis. I worked probably sixty to ninety hours a week. My student contact time was staggering. Finishing my own dissertation was difficult. I was too invested in a shadow job. After that the problems quickly proliferate. I use a pen instead of the computer. I can't even address the machine as a computer; I write "a word processor." There is a romanticism about personal style, Native Americans, and the exotics of my everyday life. The passage is eaten up with commodity fetishization. The pen appears as a subject as many times as I do. The Waterman mediates between the wildness of the Indian and the domesticated academic. What I find so glaring in the passage are personal faults like the need to be seen as different, to be as exotic as an Indian, to be as valuable as a fountain pen and as smart as Lévi-Strauss. Beneath these desires are other forces pushing me. If one can imagine the passage opening up holographically, then the hard structures of a particular biography—the house, the relationships, the geography of the small southern town—can be seen. These are the undertows pulling me to the production of the passage. On the other side of the passage are the economic forces organizing the realignment of the university and the dwindling number of jobs for an expanding number of professors. These are what make the consequences of the passage so damaging. The personal is hooked up to the structural like the trip mechanism on a bomb waiting to go off. What I produced was not just an inappropriate biography, but a wound that could be used against me.

My biography is a map in code for what will come. Lévi-Strauss stands in the center of the paragraph like John Pelham at the entrance of the cemetery. My pen is, later in the book, a spade, a shovel, a crowbar, a digging hoe, and a planchette. Behind the thin veneer of the urban landscape hinted at in the New York Public Library are the tangled Alabama woods and my grandmother's pulsating bed of asparagus. My grandfather is a door to my mother and grandmothers who aren't seen in the passage, but nevertheless hold me up. The narrow corridors among the stacks of books in the library merge with Lévi-Strauss's travels and the forced exodus of the Choctaws in the Trail of Tears to compose a layered map of passageways replete with creeks, slender deer trails, spillways, and tracings left behind in the dirt. The passage itself is like the slip of paper Poe's ruined Southern gentleman finds in the sand near a strange, heavy beetle and an ancient wreck in the story "The Gold Bug." Held up against the light, the slip of paper turns into a letter from my mother and an old photocopy in my grandfather's tuxedo and then finally into a buried dreamworld.

Three days after I handed in the sketch, there was a knock at the door. It was 6:19 p.m. I thought I was the only one still at the office. The man standing in the doorway was about six feet four. He was a senior member of the department. He leaned casually against the doorframe. He was balding and his left pant leg had ridden up over his ankle. He was wearing soft brown shoes. Discreetly inside his collar was a large wooden cross and a gold chain. "Workin' hard?" The question had an accusatory edge. "Student papers," I gestured with my pen toward the stack on the desk. "How is your dissertation coming?" The speaker's face was long. He wore a thin beard that made his mouth look like an animal crawling out of the underbrush when he talked. "Great," I lied. I was smiling. "You need to finish it if you want to stay here." He smiled and stood up straight. He must've been practicing this. "You know the biography you wrote for the newsletter? I'm the senior editor. You need to change it." And then he smoothly pointed out why. Was I sure I wanted my paragraph to look like that? Didn't I want to change from the first person to the third and change that shit about my grandfather and the Indians? Were they really necessary? I looked at the other professors' biographies. Beneath the surface there was an implicit set of directions I didn't see. Everyone else in the department followed these directions, even the author of the memo who didn't get tenure. Their biographies were all written in the third person. There was no littering of the text with extraneous details. They were written in bureaucratic prose about their past, present, and future production.

I looked at my paragraph again. The paragraph was now becoming progressively stranger, the situation more and more awkward with the editor. I thought about how Kafka's parable "Before the Law" describes a man waiting a lifetime to enter the door to the Law. I'd been waiting for years to be a professor at this college. Now that door was shutting. As the old man is dying, he asks the guard: Why has no one else come to be admitted? The guard replies, as the door shuts, Because this door was for you and you alone. I grew up with a similar story from the Gospel involving the disciple Thomas. Thomas wasn't there the first time Jesus appeared to the disciples after coming back from the dead transformed. I won't believe unless I can put my fingers into the wounds where the spikes pierced his hands and my hand into the side where he was struck with the spear.

A week later Jesus appeared to the disciples and placed Thomas's hand and fingers into his wounds, saying to him, "Doubt no longer. Believe." The Gospel is silent on whether Thomas's hands were now red with blood. In the dreamworld of Alabama I imagine Jesus' dead body stretched out like a buck on the hood of a truck. He hasn't just been shot in the abdomen; the wound in his side is a gaping hole made by a large-caliber-rifle shot, and his body has been mangled. The crown of thorns cuts into his head, just as if they were antlers pulled out from his skeleton into the air. The ropes have cut deep straps into his limbs. His back and flanks are crisscrossed with cuts from a Taiwanese hunting knife. He looks like a bloody Rosetta stone. The body is dumped at the meat processing plant, drenched in beer. And then the first miracle—after three days, he comes back to life. The wounds close. The second miracle is perhaps even more remarkable. Some wounds don't close. They remain open and are fitted to Thomas's hands and his hands alone—no one else touches Jesus—just as if they were the bullet and the ropes that killed him because this dreamworld is fitted for him and him alone.

The Mark on the Spade

I have long, indeed for years, played with the idea of setting out the sphere of life—bios—graphically on a map. First I envisioned an ordinary map, but now I would incline to a general staff's map of a city center, if such a thing existed. Doubtless it does not, because of ignorance of the theater of future wars. I have evolved a system of signs, and on the grey background of such maps they would make a colorful show.

—Walter Benjamin, "A Berlin Chronicle"

You can locate my house on a topographical map, butted up against the foothills of the Appalachian Mountains in the northeast corner of Alabama. There it is, a small square next to the intersection of White's Gap Road and Nance's Creek Road. Like the small lakes within a half mile to the south and west and the swamp off to the southeast, the house was a landmark that could be identified in aerial photographs taken in the 1950s. Before that it was known as the Big House in the valley. A yeoman farmer named Burton built the house in 1834. Burton probably came from Virginia or the Carolinas in one of the early western movements for cheaper land. He was dead by 1864. The house is identified on a Confederate military map as the Widow Burton House. All through the valley, houses were identified in this way—the Widow Lusk, the Widow Champion. Nance's Creek is named after an Indian widow. My grandfather had a different naming scheme. Each pasture was named after the man he bought it from. Out across from my house was the Barnwell pasture. Behind me on the rise was the Warlick pasture. These names didn't stick. With the same land in the hands of my father and uncle, the pastures became feminine again. The Barnwell pasture is named Mary Jane Acres after my dead mother and is broken into detailed, acre-sized plots for sale. My uncle inadvertently remembers my dead grandmother in one of his real estate swindles, naming the road into the development after her favorite flower—Cosmos Drive. My grandfather is shrunk to the size of the road sign "Shelton Farm Road" on the dirt road heading to his one-story ranch house. A chicken farmer lives there now.

The valley surrounding my house is an old war zone. Because of the mountains to the east and back to the north and west, my farm is set in a long channel running north from the Piedmont region in the south to Sand Mountain and Chattanooga, Tennessee. The flat pastures and rich bottomland were cut by State Highway 9 running north to south over dirt roads and trails dating back to the sixteenth century. In the 1940s South American fire ants arrived. All across the ruined pastures you can see their foot-high dirt mounds. They can kill a calf. Kick a mound over and you can smell the acid in the air. Hundreds of years earlier, de Soto and his army snaked up the Quataquilla Valley a half mile to the east looking for gold. The Indian wars climaxed in 1812 when Andrew Jackson crushed the Creek Indians in the Battle of Horseshoe Bend,

seventy miles to the south. Davy Crockett was part of that expedi-
tion. Jackson's troops bivouacked seven miles from my house next
to a spring I used to eat lunch at. The mountains five miles to the
east were the war zone between the Creek and Cherokee nations.
The Trail of Tears removed the last of the Creeks. Arrowheads are
easy to find after a hard rain washes across the hillside. I picked up
a sackful in an hour.

The Civil War killed the sons of the men who removed the
Creeks. My house is something they left behind. Military casualties
decimated the yeoman farmers in the valley. The Depression was
the next big wave to hit, driving the poor whites out and killing the
last of the cotton fields. No more labor to swing hoes. It was during
the Depression that a man named Warlick bought the house at auc-
tion for $112. He built a big mule barn out of heart pine below the
house. He moved his mistress into the house. Then he began the
real work. There were rumors of Indian gold buried on the land. He
dug the place up looking for treasure. He found a box of Confederate money under the stairs but that only pissed him off. The cash
was worth nothing. In 1951 an Indian who made his living following the Trail of Tears with a metal detector dug up a box during the
night directly across from Warlick's bedroom. Warlick must have
been huddled under the quilts because he never heard a thing. The
Indian made off with the gold. He left the hole uncovered for the
old man to see. After that Warlick disappeared. Whether he died or
moved away my grandfather could not remember. He bought the
land from the bank and moved in his hired hand John Parker. All
this happened four years before I was born. Property was cheap in
1951. The valley was deserted.

Just after the beginning of the new millennium, property values are booming. The valley is becoming a bedroom community. Houses are springing up as tiny ranchettes on an acre or two in the former cow pastures on top of what were pine woods at the beginning of the twentieth century. The barn that Warlick built is still standing, slowly being strangled by mud and dock weed. The broad pine boards are popping back into space. The tin roof flutters against the joists like a fat moth stuck through its abdomen with a needle. At night the tin sounds like an animal wrangling in pain.

I have a photograph of myself, the barn, and my son taken in 1989. The photo shows me pushing Tyree around the yard in a red wheelbarrow. He is two years old, bald, wearing overalls, and concentrating on something outside the frame. He looks like Napoleon surveying the battlefield. I am leaning slightly into the wheelbarrow's arms. My straw cowboy hat partially hides my face. I have just come in from stringing barbed wire. There is a rip across the thigh of my blue jeans. In the far right corner of the photo, you can catch a glimpse of the big barn hunkered down in the canopy of oak trees. It stares back like a dog. On the other side behind the camera's perspective is the house. The house wants something back from Warlick and Burton that it expects me to pay. Just within the right side of the frame is a fire ant mound. I would pound it with Amdro to poison the queen. Above it is a bare fig tree. My wife sawed the tree down when I moved out. She should have used the mattock to chop the roots, but instead she used the Swedish bow saw to whisk through the wood, leaving the trunks to rot like pieces of broken teeth in the gum line.

My family's history is tangled up in this legacy of twitching knots left behind in the ground. I might as well dig an arrowhead or a rusty steel trap out of my own fat as to pull out of the ground the grub-shaped hurt between Tyree's mother and me. The pain is expressed in categories of markings—such as the scars on my hands and arms, barbed wire, ruts in the ground, a lilac bush, a rotten stump—left behind on every surface—person, object, landscape—a historical mudslide with psychic etchings under pressure. The valley is an animate fossil tracking me down for installation in the sediment. I suppose this is the repayment the house was after.

In his history of the prison, Michel Foucault makes possible seeing these marks as part of the deployment of prison-like body regimes into daily life. Barbed wire and survey lines are part of a disciplining grid that cuts back onto the person in scars, mortgages, and anxiety. Foucault does not describe these kinds of marks directly, though he comes close. In his opening description of the execution of Damiens before a crowd gathered in the Paris streets, the man is first pruned back and then his roots are cut out of him like the fig tree in my yard. He is systematically torn apart, each piece corresponding algebraically to the King's power until he blooms in sprays of blood and his organs are turned out in vivid displays of summer color. At the end of the spectacle there is a dog curled asleep on the warm spot left from burning his body to ashes. Not a single mark or moment, but a spectrum of timed marks are a part of a scriptural economy through which power is organized into convulsive fields or landscapes. Foucault uses Damiens to chart the shift in corporal spectacles to the new organization of power exemplified in the prison architecture of the panoptic. The other way to follow the shift is to point out that Foucault moves from the body as a landscape to the reform house as a larger landscape made up of individually marked bodies, not unlike a colony of organized microbes on a tongue depressor or a stand of ruthlessly hoed corn.

Indeed, this is the direction of his history in *Discipline and Punish*. He starts with a body, moves to a change in marking technologies—the sword is replaced by the guillotine, and the corresponding transition from the street to the prison and its kin, the factory, the hospital, and the school. The body and the person are separate landscapes fitted inside each other. Smaller landscapes are slid like Chinese boxes into other landscapes, like Freud's wallet inside his coat pocket fitted within his office, fitted inside the corner of his house set in a fashionable neighborhood at the end of the Austro-Hungarian Empire. The French historian Fernand Braudel called these fittings "a set of sets."

> It is with this in mind and for want of a better term, that I have come to think of society as a "set of sets," the sum of all the things that historians encounter in the various branches of our research. I am borrowing from mathematics a concept so convenient that mathematicians themselves distrust it; and I am perhaps using rather a grand word (in French the word for set is ensemble, which also means "whole") to underline the obvious truth that everything under the sun is, and cannot escape being, social. But the point of a definition is to provide an approach to a problem, to lay down some guidelines for preliminary observation. If it makes that observation easier, both at the beginning and in later stages, if it helps to produce an acceptable classification of the material and to develop the logic of the argument, then the definition is useful and has justified itself. If we use the expression "set of sets" or "ensemble des ensembles," does this not usefully remind us that any given social reality we may observe in isolation is in itself contained in some greater set; that as a collection of variables, it requires and implies the existence of other collections of variables outside itself?[1]

Markings move from the smallest social unit to the largest, reinforcing each unit in an escalating habitus in which the structures percolate from the deep unconscious interior onto the muscle and fat, onto the skin, across the Made in China tag, to the posture and commodity assemblage. The scriptural economy is pervasive, scrambling traditional boundaries between the social and organic. "Imagine," Bruno Latour writes, "a study that would treat the ozone hole as simultaneously naturalized, sociologized and deconstructed?"[2]

The house is two stories tall with enormous chimneys on the east and west sides. There is a double-decker porch smack in the center dividing the house into thirds. It occupies the intersection of the house like a prosthetic ornament designed to produce a formal elegance. I used to sit there with Tyree and watch Japanese trucks buzz by at sixty miles an hour. Neither of the doors to the porch works. The porch is now starting to wrench free from the boards against the house, lured by car wrecks to twist on the nails and screws. On either side are the distinctive nine-over-six windows. The individual panes were handblown—at least that is what my grandfather told me. The roof is tin. It is the same color as the barn roof. A weather vane and a lightning rod system installed in 1890 run across the top of the house. The doors are what is known as open Bible style. The panels crossing the tongue-and-groove boards reproduce an open Bible in a kind of wooden literacy. The original door to the upstairs bedrooms from the back was outside on the porch, which is why a meat hook hangs from the ceiling. Salt pork must have hung there. The house is a modified saltbox with a one-story addition cropped onto the frame. It is the oldest standing house in the county, though that doesn't mean a damn. Just an old house painted gray, flanked on one side by a pecan orchard, on the other side by white pines and spreading shrubs, with a rundown pasture split by a small creek running down the back side.

The creek bank swarms with willows and alders. The watercourse hasn't changed noticeably in forty years, but you can still see in the ground where the water used to run. There are the cuts in the ground that housed the creek channel. Just under the thin layer of grass, the ground is clogged with rocks. In *A Thousand Years of Nonlinear History,* Manuel De Landa describes a river as a sorting machine to get at how hierarchies of sediment and muck are formed:

> Geologists have discovered one such mechanism: rivers acting as veritable hydraulic computers (or, at least, a sorting machine). Rivers transport rocky materials from their point of origin (eroding mountain) to the bottom of the ocean, where these materials accumulate. In the course of this process, pebbles of various size, weight, and shape react differently to the water transporting them. Some are so small they dissolve in the water; some are larger and are carried in suspension; even larger stones move by jumping back and forth from the river bed to the streaming water, while the largest ones are moved by traction as they roll along the bottom toward their destination. The intensity of the river flow (i.e., its speed and other intensities such as temperature or clay saturation) also determines the outcome, since a large pebble that can only be rolled by a moderate current may be transported in suspension by a powerful eddy. (Since there is feedback between pebble properties and flow properties, as well as between the river and its bed, the "sorting computer" is clearly a highly nonlinear dynamic system).[3]

What De Landa means by this is more than a description led by a suggestive metaphor. De Landa cuts back on the notion of social stratification: "The term social strata is itself clearly a metaphor, involving the idea that, just as geological strata are layers of rocky materials stacked on top of each other, so classes and castes are layers—some higher, lower—of human materials." He asks, "Is it possible to go beyond the metaphor and show that the genesis of both geological and social strata involves the same engineering diagram?" (59). When he writes this, he's not just making a linguistic analogy; rather, he's saying that rivers embody the same diagrams used by engineers and teachers as little engineers to build a school that separates and sorts students by class, intelligence, and gender. Rivers and institutions both work as sorting machines in the creation and maintenance of hierarchies. De Landa puts the ground under our feet into the historical process. The formation of creeks and pastures is tied to conventional historical accounts such as the transformation of Burton's cotton fields into cow pastures in the 1940s. Each stage of economic development reorganizes the landscape and the ecological system. But just beyond the effects of rivers and cow hooves and the concretization of social hierarchies is the formation of an acid-like fog, at once nostalgic and capital-intensive, that condenses on structures and begins a corrosive process. Nostalgia and capital investments follow the same channels cut into the landscape as the Black Angus cows.

History is a set of flows that sorts and cuts the ground under our feet. Like an enormous tableau the landscape around my small square farmhouse is etched and scratched in different languages by different tools and animal assemblage. The swamps and the large leaf pines gave way to cotton fields and hoes, then to open pastures and grazing cows, and were finally overtaken by chicken houses and ranchettes with golden retrievers shitting in the concrete kennels in the back. Freud wrote about these connections to describe the nostalgic feelings his friend had looking out over the ocean:

> It is a feeling which he would like to call the sensation of "eternity," a feeling as of something limitless, unbounded—as it were, "oceanic." This feeling, he adds, is a purely subjective fact, not an article of faith; it brings with it no assurance of personal immortality, but it is the source of the religious energy which is seized upon by the various Churches and religious systems, directed by them into particular channels, and doubtless also exhausted by them.[4]

Freud's answer to the origin of this feeling is a memory of the mother's breast. De Landa's river is not so far from Freud's water machine for memory. Freud's breast is at least 80 percent water. The river, like a breast, sorts and divides desires into oedipal sediments. Freud sews together a postal network overseen by the state (he receives the expression of the nostalgia in a letter from his friend), a tender nostalgia in the aftermath of a rail trip to the beach, and a breast pumping milk. Here is a whole series of what Deleuze and Guattari describe as a machine, scratched into an emotional substructure as expansive as any landscape: "The breast is a machine that produces milk, and the mouth a machine coupled to it. The mouth of the anorexic wavers between several functions: its possessor is uncertain as to whether it is an eating machine, an anal machine, a talking machine, or a breathing machine."[5]

Within ten paces of the house was another building. Squared off at seventeen feet by seventeen feet, it is too small to have been a barn. I found what must have been the hearth straight back from the door underneath four short pine boards. A red clay, handmade brick was half buried in the soft black dirt. The brick was the last survivor;

the others were pillaged years back. The outbuilding shares similar architectural features with the house—post and beam construction, pegs, square-headed nails, and clapboard. The handyman John Parker told me the building was the original kitchen. He was seventy-three years old, a scrawny, rawboned figure barely able to keep his overalls on. He always wore a white T-shirt that stuck to him like a rag soaked in kerosene. "Could it have been slave quarters?" I asked.

"Shit naw. Kitchen."

My grandfather A. C. Shelton—the initials were like columns stuck on a plain name—added shed roofs off three sides into the adjoining pasture, where the bulls could get some shade and lick salt blocks. They churned the ground up. And after they were gone, the dirt turned into a fine, dried dust several inches deep. Like something from a pharaoh's dream, the shed floor was covered with a field of antlion pyramids swirled into the powder. At the bottom of these cones were the enormous jaws of the larvae. The *Audubon Field Guide* gives this brief description:

> Often known as doodlebugs, the larvae have oversize heads with long spiny jaws, short legs, and bristles all over their bodies. Most hide at the bottom of small pit traps made in the sand and wait for ants and other small insects to tumble down the sloping sides. The larvae in some species do not build pits but lie buried in sand or hide among debris waiting for prey. The pupation occurs in a parchmentlike cocoon buried in the sand. The adult emerges from the cocoon through an opening cut in one end, leaving the conical door still in place as though hinged. Antlions are most common in the South and Southwest, where larva pits can be seen in most places with dry sandy soil.[6]

My grandfather is dead, himself the victim of a voracious descent. Goffman wrote of a "betrayal funnel"[7] to describe the gradual collapse of the social relationships around the asylum patient, as if they really were made of sand with a creature curled just out of sight. In prehistoric periods dragonflies were three feet long. What size did their larvae get? The size of the nurse who ran down the hall screaming, "Stop him," as Granddad shuffled across the linoleum toward the exit. He starved himself to death in a nursing home after a series of small strokes left him slightly out of his mind and unable to control his bladder. Behind this were a series of real estate deals initiated by my uncle. The farm was sold off.

I dreamed I saw my grandfather floating underwater in the big lake with the Amur, grass-eating carp from Vietnam, cruising alongside him. These are torpedo-shaped seventy-pound fish. A clump of algae was curled around his foot. The surface of the lake was sealed with a see-through Tupperware cover. I stood on the surface looking down at him and the fish, wondering if the fish would bruise his white skin. Ten years before he died, Granddad sold real estate to support his sons' business dealings. I would drive him around the county in his blue Plymouth filled with baling twine, medicine, corn, newspapers, a tattoo kit, buckets, and his walking stick. He pointed out to me how the Arabs were buying up giant tracts of pasture and pine forests. What he did not see was how his fish were part of a water compass reoriented toward Kublai Khan's old dream palace.

The shed is an elephant's graveyard. Time is slowed down to the speed of rust. The tools are parts of old families reaching back into the past for ancestors. Only their concurrence is modern. Objects, like an old iron bed frame and a collection of ladder-back chairs that no longer have a place inside, wait here, stuffed in the corners, hanging from nails. There is a one-hundred-pound anvil salvaged from the collapsed blacksmith shop a hundred fifty paces into the pecan orchard. There are cotton bale scales. Wooden boxes filled with tools sit patiently for Jesus to come back with their dead. My bee equipment—veils, helmets, frames, and an extractor—has a place in the corner. There are old horse bridles and mule yokes with dirt dauber nests affixed to them draped over the ceiling joists. Rats have crisscrossed the soft ground beneath the floorboards. Termites have turned the corner posts to sponge held up by nails. Wasps float across the room like German zeppelins over London.

I kept my tools in here hung up on ten-penny nails. In the center was my English spade with a filled D handle. The blade was sharp enough to cut a snake in two like a noodle. Hanging in a line were a hard rake and two solid strap forks forged in England, identical to each other except for one broken tine. Then there was a Felco pruner made in Switzerland; Japanese hedge clippers; an Austrian and a Japanese hoe, both American pattern; and a Coleman hoe. Propped against the wall were a grubbing mattock with a full seven-pound head in the shape of a dinosaur head and a railroad pick I inherited from my granddad A. C. Shelton. Standing were two forged Irish heart-shaped shovels, one made in America and the other in England, and a red enameled watering can. The tools sat next to each other like volumes in an international encyclopedia set. There is a strange concurrence of language here that is neither English nor Japanese but a cutting dialect. These tools are devoted to cutting rhizomic grasses, disciplining spreading shrubs, and chopping dirt. A garden is a monumental corpse made of foliage and dirt, a breathing, eating statue with a different appetite than the war memorials in the nearby town. My tools carve living marble into monuments that harbor bees and fleas.

Over the spade was a dogwood root mallet I made from a tree near where the Widow Champion is buried. She died in 1842. The Widow Champion's grave is a small plot hidden in the woods. Oaks and hickories grow right through her. The space used to be a clearing, but the house site has been swallowed. There is no trace of the rock foundation. The widow's grave is the only one with a cut stone identifying who she was. The others are hard to account for exactly. There are possibly seven other bodies under the ground here, identified by stacks of two or three rocks piled on one end as a headstone and on the other as a footstone. The space in between has sunk, leaving a concave mark in the ground like a heavy body lying on top of the soft leaves. The widow is the queen of these spaces in her death. My cousins hatched a plan to dig her up at night. It was romantic, almost like a date. Her body, in their minds, was like an Egyptian mummy wrapped in what now would be an imaginary shirt. She would be naked to the bone. You would be able to see straight through her hips and breastbone to a thin veneer of black humus on red clay. On her left hand would be a gold ring. Her skull would stare back like Nefertiti looking for her skin suit. I watched them scratch at the ground for forty minutes under the glare of a big flashlight. The hickory roots and the rocks woven into a dense pubic thicket across the surface of the grave stopped the dig. Their shovels were too dull to cut through them. None of them knew how to use either a file or a mattock.

Then there are an English bush ax, a swing blade with a serrated edge, crosscut saws, hammers of all kinds, axes, mauls, wedges, and a ditch spade with my grandfather's thumbprint etched into the wood. I used this spade when I dug the ditch for the cable TV line from the street through the eleagnus hedge to the house. It hangs near the middle of the rack next to a pitchfork and a four-foot level. It belonged to my grandfather on my mother's side. He died when I was less than a year old. He called me "blue eyes." Along the grip there is an indentation caused by a thumb rubbing the wood. My grandmother gave me the spade. She was the gardener; he kept bees and played croquet. The thumb mark could be hers or Henry's, the black hired hand who worked for her occasionally. I fantasize it is my grandfather's. I like to ease my thumb into the space as if I were resetting a molar deep in someone's mouth, placing my thumb in the gap like a new tooth filling in the absence with a reverence of absence. The mark is an opening to my dead grandfather's hand. On the other side is the callus on my thumb. At the time I could pick up hot coals that had spilled out from the wood stove with my bare hands.

If my grandfather's spade is marked by absence, my garden is stuffed with creamy white grubs and rusty pieces of metal. Luke Coppick, who grew up in the house, told me that when he was a kid he used to play in what they thought were the slave quarters. Directly behind the house was an outhouse, but there wasn't any hole in the ground. If there ever was a hole, it had filled up a long time ago. The ground was hard-packed when I tore down the outhouse in 1980. The outhouse jumped straight up, the sloped roof facing south. A small peach tree curled around it underneath the shade of a giant pecan tree. It came down easily. A sledgehammer to the four-by-four corner, and it disappeared like a dummy through a trapdoor in a stage show.

Coppick never told me what the quarters looked like. He said the word "quarters" like that was dimension enough. But across the street he pointed toward a deserted farm shack. "Over there," he gestured, "I saw the ghost of an old man dressed in overalls and a straw hat. He was there one second talking to me, and then he was just gone."

"My mother thought that house was haunted. She saw a man standing by the well," I said while screwing my eyes into the space. I wanted to see the man.

Coppick picked up speed. "My wife was driving the car. I was walking along the side of the road raking up the hay where the county had mowed. This old farmer was standing there. I threw an armful of hay into the trunk. Then he was just gone, like he was raptured. Loraine never saw nothing. She told me I had a heat stroke or something."

Coppick was making a map for me to garden by.[8] I imagined that these quarters, now completely disappeared from my garden plot, somehow have changed the flavor of the tomatoes. The map didn't locate the assassin bugs or the red-clay bottoms; it is the opposite of marble and how that rock is made into monuments. Coppick's map was gestural, sliced psychic cuttings made with an Old Henry pocketknife, a two-blade, bone-handle knife with a sticky pull. Coppick's landmarks are delicate and translucent tissues nestled into the air. It was 1910 when he played in the slave quarters out back. He never mentioned where the outhouse was. "That there was the kitchen. Over there were two slave houses. My bedroom was the room upstairs on the east. We slept on the upstairs porch in the summer. We moved out in 1917." On the wall by the door young Coppick scrawled the time he left his home. I found the line vibrating like an abscessed tooth just beneath a thin layer of buttermilk paint. My wife quietly reburied it beneath a cream-colored latex paint. Coppick's family moved one-half mile down the road to a house constructed out of rough-cut pine boards.

"That was your house on the hill over there?" I pointed to the top of the hill a quarter mile away in the direction of Nance's Creek. There was a pile of flat rocks overgrown with grasses where the house had been.

"Yeah. We raised cotton. The house burned down. We came in for lunch. Mama was baking biscuits. The chimney caught on fire." He remembered the history like a grocery list.

"You had a chimney fire?" My hand was jammed into my jeans pocket.

"Shoot. The chimney was shooting fire. The damn thing fell apart. The house burned up so fast we couldn't even get on our shoes. Mama made us take 'em off before we could come in."[9] He smacked his lips as he spoke. "The damn thing was so hot. The mud fell out between the rocks."

Coppick puts together a geography of vanishing points. The disappeared hoes, an old man in overalls, his mama's house, the cotton fields, the slave quarters, the kitchen, and the slaves are like ghost vessels cruising beneath the surface. Coppick lives now in a one-story brick house, no fireplace. His daughter and her husband live next door.[10] They both work for the city. Behind his house is a Quonset hut where he had a workshop. He and his wife devoted a block of their savings to send their daughter to a good school and then to medical school. She quit after two years.

If I were to try to draw out this map on the very ground that he described, I would have to find a portion of the surface of my farm that is perfectly level and smooth. To construct a map, the piece of ground would have to be measured and inscribed either by the eye or with a string and a framing square. The grass would need to be removed with a flat edge of the spade to the depth of at least two inches to get at the shallow roots. The grass cut, the first trench of the map can be dug to a depth of ten inches deep and ten inches wide. The dirt is shoveled into a wheelbarrow and rolled to the end of the map to fill in the last trench. Once the first trench is dug, a roll of grass is cut and placed grass side down on the bottom. This will improve the soil. Then in sequence, going backward, each trench line is cut and lifted into the blank space on top of the face-down grass. Care should be taken not to turn the soil over to preserve its composition. At the end the dirt in the wheelbarrow is dumped in the last trench line. The ground should be chopped with a hoe and raked clear of all rocks and weeds. Then turning the rake over to its flat face, smooth out the straited cuts left by the rake's teeth. Draw the map. But now suppose that our resemblance is to be made absolutely exact. A map of my farm, contained within my farm, to represent, down to the minutest detail, every contour and marking, natural or artificial, that occurs upon the surface of the farm. "For the map, in order to be complete, according to the rule given, will have to contain, as a part of itself, a representation of its own contour and contents. In order that this representation should be constructed, the representation itself will have to contain once more, as a part of itself, a representation of its own contour and contents; and this representation, in order to be exact, will have once more to contain an image of itself; and so on without limit,"[11] until his hand touching my hand is lost in the infinitely receding humus.

There is physicality to the absence Coppick points out. My garden, like Freud's Rome, is one layer in an archaeological site, reaching back through John Parker's hard-packed outhouse to the slaves, to the Indian squash fields prior to 1830. I dig up hand-made square-head nails, steel traps, glass bottles, boot soles, and an occasional bone.[12] What I can't dig up, I can feel in the stories Coppick told to put his fantasies into absence. There is tactility to these fantasies of absence. The body is habituated to the spade, forming a new actant on a site older than the televisual. The body is still plugged into a seasonal, mimetic technology. It is slower. In the fall, yellow and black garden spiders the size of half-dollars suck grasshoppers stuck in their webs. The garden uses ghosts like the slave quarters and the old kitchen as penetrating tools. The intangible itself becomes a televisual coffin to project fantasies back toward Coppick. Like Coppick's tenant family, the slave quarters have melted into the ground. There is no way to know if the nail dug up or the old ax head has anything to do with the absence. Like the marks on the spade handle, there is no way to reconstruct the body behind it. There is the fantasy of the touch of another's hand and of the sharpness of the pieces of broken blue glass swimming in the dirt. There is the risk of cutting your hand reaching into the dirt. Underneath the map, the soft ground would attract earthworms and moles who would trace in their burrowings a double to the map's surface.

The buildings moved like a migrating bird that never returns. The buildings exist as a waking dream[13] that wants Coppick even though the quarters may not have existed at all. Coppick doesn't arrive on the scene until after 1910. It's unlikely that the shoddily constructed quarters would have persisted for over forty years or more. Maybe. Maybe Coppick's ghosted building could be traced to a more immediate racialized history. He supported George Wallace.

At his home in town, he would stand in the front yard and eyeball across Ladiga Street at the black part of town barely two hundred yards away. "You know," he said. "We all use to call it Needmore. Now it's the Eastside, but it's still Needmore to me."

Nothing was simple or direct about Coppick. He may have been putting together an ironic commentary, or his talk could be considered wrapped around what Steven Dubin terms symbolic slavery. "How have blacks and other minority groups been kept in symbolic servitude by the repetition of particular images in mass-produced items? Taken collectively, do such items comprise a code which has contributed to the replication of majority-minority relations? If so, recording these relations in material form provides a template to continue to organize actual social relations in specific ways."[14] Dubin's answer points to the everyday objects like lawn jockeys, cookie jars, postcards, or the ghosted slave quarters that make up Coppick's world. Dubin describes a racist nostalgia that attaches itself to hard artifacts like lawn jockeys,[15] but his concept could just as easily be applied to ghost structures. Coppick clings nostalgically to a world in which he was white trash but in which the codes of whiteness still absolve him.

Under the same pecan tree that shaded the outhouse, John Parker would sit in a straight-back chair and stare at his grandson tied to the trunk like Fay Wray waiting for King Kong. "Goddamn him," he'd say. "He gets away from me." Flies would light on Parker's hat[16] and hunker down like it was made of flesh. Parker worked for my granddad. He signed his name with an X. He trapped. In a room in the house he dried animal tails from a clothesline. His wife beat him with an iron frying pan. He had two daughters and a son. He wore overalls and half boots. Altogether he could not have weighed more than 130 pounds. His son-in-law murdered his youngest daughter. She weighed 300 pounds. It was nearly a week before anyone found her body, like a big slab of melting butter, on the living room floor. The other daughter was named Rachel. She looked like Dolly Parton in a brown wig. She collected antiques from the mill village and liked to belly dance. My wife and I were at her house looking at her collection when suddenly she put on a Middle Eastern record, picked up a long silk scarf, and shimmied her ass across the room. "I love to dance." It was bizarrely beautiful. The son took Polaroids of topless women posing next to his Chevy truck. The truck was red. Only Rachel and her mother Opal ever came back to visit the house they lived in most of their lives.

Directly opposite where Parker would sit I planted a lilac at the edge of the shade. Parker had a sitting style. He would sit straight up in a ladder-back chair for an instant, and then he would lean forward into an aerodynamic tuck with his elbows on his knees and his legs cobbled out. No chair, he fell into a hunker with his small ass hovering inches from the ground and his knees stuck into a V. John Parker didn't care much for flowers or figs. He loved cornbread and fried meat. He would not have noticed the lilac that has taken his place under the pecan. I dug the lilac up out of my mother's yard. She got it from her mother, who got it from her mother's mother. My grandmother was already dead when I planted the lilac, but I see it as a gift from her. Eleven feet to the southwest is a row of jaggedly stacked rocks from the pasture running in a line for eight paces with an arm curling north toward what the Victorian fairy tale writer George MacDonald called the land behind the north wind, which is where the dead go to wait for Christ. Under this arm looking north,[17] I buried a malamute. Each section in the line is a grave filled with dogs and cats. The graves are two and a half feet deep, straight sides, smoothed with a flat spade, packed dirt. I stomp on them to pack the dirt. I pile rocks on top to keep dogs from digging up the carcass. A winter honeysuckle spreads across the intersection of the arm and the line.

Early on in *Civilization and Its Discontents,* Freud makes an analogy between Rome and the mind. "Now let us, by a flight of imagination, suppose that Rome is not a human habitation but a psychical entity with a similarly long and copious past." He is struggling to come up with an image to conceptualize how the mind retains traces of its past in buried or repressed, half-remembered psychic accumulation beneath the present. It is a typical surrealist move for Freud, predicated on an urban scaffolding. Inside of buildings are the remains of previous structures. "It is hardly necessary to remark that all these remains of ancient Rome are found dovetailed into the jumble of a great metropolis which is grown up in the last few centuries since the Renaissance. There is certainly not a little that is ancient still buried in the soil of the city or beneath its modern buildings. This is the manner in which the past is preserved in historical sites like Rome."[18]

He pushed the comparison further. Memory surfaces in odd aches at the tender parts of the body like snakes rippling across the imperceptible spaces between the muscle and the skin. Nothing that has once come into existence or that has passed away in earlier phases of development can escape this Rome. "This would mean that in Rome the palaces of the Caesars . . . would still be rising to their old height on the Palatine and that the castle of S. Angelo would still be carrying on its battlements the beautiful statues which graced it until the siege by the Goths, and so on."[19] It is an unconscious empire. The mind retains its past, even as the new debris accumulates, sending shivers across the surface of the skin.

Freud's equation can be indefinitely extended to the child's wax tablet of the "Mystic Writing-Pad":

> Some time ago there came upon the market, under the name of the Mystic Writing-Pad, a small contrivance that promises to perform more than the sheet of paper or the slate. It claims to be nothing more than a writing-tablet from which notes can be erased by an easy movement of the hand. But if it is examined more closely it will be found that its construction shows a remarkable agreement with my hypothetical structure of our perceptual apparatus and that it can in fact provide both an ever-ready receptive surface and permanent traces of the notes that have been made upon it.[20]

Or as I do, to a garden sprawling around a house. The advantage of shifting the comparison from the public structure of the city to the child's pad or the garden is that immediately the simile is put in touch with the oedipal triangle in the household. The degrees of movement are more constrained. The holes into the unconscious are more intimately accessible. In the end, the mystic writing pad is a smaller, more portable Rome. Freud is left with an interlocking urban landscape that traces the mind from the smallest unit—a toy—to the grand architecture of the city. But Freud's landscape is suspect from the very beginning. His map lacks a rhizomic, or floral,[21] intelligence. The garden, absent from Freud's mapping, acts as an intermediary in between these interlocking structures. The garden adds insects and green snakes peeking out of the roses and thorns, emphasizing that the optical unconscious is more than the sofas, dens, and mimetic technologies Benjamin imagined—it teems.

> Evidently a different nature opens itself to the camera than opens to the naked eye—if only because an unconsciously penetrated space is substituted for a space consciously explored by man. Even if one has a general knowledge of the way people walk, one knows nothing of a person's posture during the fractional second of a stride. The act of reaching for a lighter or a spoon is familiar routine, yet we hardly know what really goes on between hand and metal, not to mention how this fluctuates with our moods. Here the camera intervenes with the resources of its lowerings and liftings, its interruptions and isolations, its extensions and accelerations, its enlargements and reductions. The camera introduces us to unconscious optics as does psychoanalysis to unconscious impulses.[22]

The garden is a border between a series of interlocked structures, which are twined together like honeysuckle around a sapling. The bare branch stretched like a network of arms about to bud across the kitchen window. The flat, white cut of the pruner visible on the branches, a red wagon turned on its side on a gravel path, through the glass to a bowl of Honey Nut Cheerios and an Oneida spoon. The garden retains a history and the accumulation of debris and markings on the ground. The spade cut, the pruned branch, the scar on the hand, the rotting compost retains the compositional structure of Freud's simile but gives it a more personal, smaller radius. The garden stands for an arboresque and more human vegetative mind alongside Freud's metropolitan equation. The intertwining of the family with the commercial and bureaucratic triangles begins as soon as the doorknob is turned and the man mistakes his wife for a straw hat. At the same time a floral surrealism blooms in the margins. Instead of following streets and monuments in an archaeological dig, the garden simile develops the lilac into a new patient for analysis. The lilac has a history that is personal as well as genetic. It is an actant with stories to tell. The lilac talks in the same language as the unconscious connected to the Irish shovel connected to the habituation of the body parts at the end of the ash handle. The commodity trails meld with dreams to make possible a new archaeology that Freud didn't quite see. There is still the repressed. A Kafka-like mother and father lurking in the background, but the garden is a different kind of oedipal site. Plants, objects, and bodies are not separate but are wrapped systems with stories originating as much out of the actant as the actor. The shovel gardens. The gardener is another tool in an oedipal archaeology. The garden acts for me as Rome did for Freud or Paris did for Walter Benjamin. I am put in touch with catastrophes and loneliness as poignant as the smell of lilac in the landscape.

Juluka was one of the dogs buried in the rocks under the winter honeysuckle. He died while I was teaching in Iowa. He was a Hungarian guard dog, a Kuvasz I had raised from a pup. My mother hired Blackie, a character from down the road, to bury the dog. He complained about how hard the ground was. It had to be picked. The grave was too shallow; the dogs scrabbled the rocks away after a rat. They dug up the carcass. A single paw stuck up in the air like Excalibur. I hauled dirt in and reburied Juluka in a mound, pounding the dirt and laying thirty-pound rocks on top.

I buried Juluka as if he were a tree going into the ground. The hole for his grave had to be two and a half times his size. Peat moss is traditionally added to lighten the soil and increase moisture absorption.

By the time I had him in the ground, rigor mortis had him spread out. The hole had to be as wide as he was tall unless I broke his legs at the joints. I fitted him in the ground, taking care not to drop him in the hole. I placed my straw hat over his face so that the dirt wouldn't get in his eyes. My son, Tyree, knows the names of these animals that he's never seen. "There's Martin Luther, Tara, Eli, Juluka, Diva." I would say this as if they were alive and would come if I called. Tyree is schooled in the supernatural. Before he was born, I wrote a poem about him. The central images are me piling up brush to burn, the small deaths between his mother and me, and calling out his name across the orchard. The final image twists on his never being born and the oedipal archaeology that digs and configures the garden. My garden works off the pulses of absences and presence of fathers and mothers. Plant a shrub; mark a tool with my thumb. The reconstruction of the family is another layer in the strata that pervade the soil. The ghosted slave quarters, the rusted nails, the broken pieces of blue glass, and the projections into my son coexist in the dirt with a thin layer of humus. The deep red clay, the creamy white grubs congeal into a surrealist alternative to the metropolis.

At the corner of the fence on the southwest side of the pecan shade I am treeing a wisteria vine. Wisteria came from China. It blooms in the spring, thick purple clusters. It can smother a tree, strapped around the trunk like heavy rubber bands. It came to Virginia in the seventeenth century as part of the embellishment of the larger plantations. It came to Jacksonville, Alabama, in 1864 as adornment over a coffin. The gallant Pelham, an officer in the Confederate Army, had shrapnel added to his head at Kelly's Ford. His head was knocked off again in the late 1960s when it was stolen from his statue at the entrance to the city cemetery. It was made from white Italian marble. He stands with one leg slightly forward, strangely feminine looking, with a plump ass. Curls spring out from beneath his hat. His right hand rests on his sword. Behind him are rows of Confederate dead. A new head is on his shoulders now. Confederate flags are stuck in the dirt and flutter like red and blue butterflies.

At the center of the town square in Jacksonville, Alabama, a statue of a Confederate soldier stares north up the highway. The highway is named after Pelham. The Confederate soldier has no name. Instead, there is an inscription at the base of the statue describing how while men may change, values never do. I lived as a kid in an antebellum mansion on Pelham Road with my grandparents. In my memory the statue of the Confederate soldier turns on a hidden mechanical dial so that he is always facing me. He doesn't stay still in my memory as the officer does in the cemetery. He moves as I move. He is part of the fatal strategy of the Confederate state sunk into a network of memorials that can't be viewed too critically without pulling the plug on the values commemorated in the inscriptions. Ironically, the values are acknowledged as obscene themselves in the inscription. They are turned away from the eye. No values are mentioned. Only their existence and persistence is noted; it is a reverence of absence. In the gaps, and in the holes left by the omission, a line can be wound like a wisteria vine pregnant with clusters of purple blooms through the remnants of the Confederate state to the new commercial district, reorganizing and projecting the old South's residual values. The memorial is an entrance into the obscene, which in turn opens into the larger territorializations of absences hidden in the perfume of flowers.

Pelham's coffin was shipped south draped with wisteria cuttings from his lovers. I can see the wisteria through my kitchen window: a thin skeleton unbloomed in the middle of a rampage of grasses and weeds. It had been a wet spring. Tyree was kicking a soccer ball in the backyard using the graves as a goal. There are six panes in the window. In the upper left pane the purple vetch was swarming. The old glass gave the grasses a wavy quality even though the wind wasn't blowing. The winter honeysuckle fluttered in the glass like my grandmother's hair. Tyree yelled, "Daddy, play with me. You promised." "In a few minutes," I said as I came outside. The way I said "few" pulled the word into taffy, a sticky reminder of my garbled accent. "Let me finish pruning these shrubs." I pointed to winter honeysuckle spread through the pile of rocks wrapped around the line of dead pets. I had my Felco pruner in my hands, snapping them like a sharp little Swiss guillotine. I reached down into a clump of grasses to cut back a dead branch on the winter honeysuckle. I wanted a good, clean cut. The honeysuckle smell like gardenia in the late winter when they pop into a blast of tiny white flowers.

Tyree was talking to me. "Look at this, Dad. Look, look, Dad." I looked. The branch felt funny. It didn't cut like it was supposed to. It squished. I pulled my hand up. I had cut through my thumbnail to the bone. Big globs of blood oozed out onto my white T-shirt. This will never come out, I thought.

"That's cool, Dad, look at the blood." I was starting to panic. This was a big gaping cut the size of a coin purse.

"Let me see, Dad." He thought the cut was an exhibit I had put together for him. I washed the cut out, holding it under the water in the sink and pouring hydrogen peroxide over it so that it fizzed over like a Coke.

My mother called. She wanted me to go to the hospital to get stitches. "You cut yourself with a pair of pruners?" she said. "Why did you do that?"

I wondered if I should say something about April being the cruelest month. It's a question of faith, I would say, pure hard faith. If your hand offends you, cut it off.

The Abduction of Mary Janie

His face is turned toward the past. Where we perceive a chain of events, he sees one single catastrophe which keeps piling wreckage upon wreckage and hurls it in front of his feet. The angel would like to stay, awaken the dead, and make whole what has been smashed. But a storm is blowing from Paradise; . . .

—Walter Benjamin, "Theses on the Philosophy of History"

The refrigerator was a white Kenmore. It was slid into the corner at the end of the kitchen next to a window. The window had off-white curtains with delicate ruffles on a wooden rod and looked out into the pecan orchard. The trunk of the first tree looked like a man standing on the lawn looking in. On top of the refrigerator were old pop bottles that I had found in the garden and under the house—a 7-Up, a Dr Pepper, an orange soda, and an ancient Pepsi bottle shaped like an obelisk. Stuck on the door were drawings my son had done at school. The refrigerator made a little rattle when the thermostat kicked on. The only other sound came from the ceiling fan that, I remember, barely skirted the curtains. This was fifteen years ago. The fan is still there. It has a lifetime guarantee. But I'm not. The house was sold two years ago this May. The Kenmore is at the bottom of a landfill in Calhoun County. In a moment I will open the refrigerator door and where I am now will begin.

For Marcel Proust's character this moment caught in time was tinged with sweetness. He was having tea with his aunt on a quiet afternoon. As he wavered between the past and present, there were a cookie, tea, and an aunt, acting as a lifeline tethered to his hand as he slid into a world that is neither here nor there and floated like a cosmonaut in the soupy air of a bourgeois parlor. He was what H. G. Wells called a chronic Argonaut with "chronic" referring to how time is being eaten into oblivion. The tea would get cold if left unattended. His companion might grow impatient. There was a set timetable for Proust's immersion into his past that kept the experience as soft as a cookie soaked in tea. I wish it were as simple as that—sugar, flour, and butter shaped into a lost seashell. But even with Proust's tranquil scene there is a storm in the awful repetition that acts like a whirlpool whose smallest point is the cup that sucks one in and then out into an ocean of memories from which now is drawn. Benjamin's storm is no different. A single angel is drawn from the heavenly host and is being sucked down a long corridor the size of a pin made especially for him and him alone.

I grew up where the past mixed openly with the present. The line between the dead and the living was blurry. I knew my dead grandfather, Eli Landers, his hairline and smell, as if he were still here and just taking a nap behind a locked door. Over the mantle in the living room was a portrait of him. My aunt had painted the picture of Eli sitting in his study with the spines of books filling in the background. The study was revamped after his death into a holding room for stray furniture and a piano. The books were moved to the long hallway in the center of the house. His name was writ-

ten in longhand in each one. It seemed natural to associate a man
I had never met but grew up with—I saw his grave once a week—
with books. The books seemed to be from the equivalent of a prehistoric time. The pictures inside the history books were filled with
heroic bodies and tragic wrecks splintering on rocks, muscles bursting, grotesque tortures from the religious wars of the sixteenth century, and monumental calms stretched across landscapes of men
and women standing in the middle of marble, stone, and graceful,
sharp-pointed leaves. These pictures had an incalculable effect on
my own psychic skeleton. The side porch was a fortress. Geronimo
coexisted with Ivanhoe. Max Ernst, the surrealist, used the same period pieces in his collages in the 1930s. But Ernst set what was out
of joint on a piece of paper. The juxtaposition of time in my world
inside my grandmother's house was still wild. A small black-and-
white TV lounged in a room with mahogany and wicker furniture
from the 1920s. A tintype of a Confederate soldier sided with velvet,
a broken-back divan, eighty-year-old books, and what my relations
did in the Civil War lay together in unenforced collages.

My mother's mother's name was Pearl Baskin Landers. Her
father was a country doctor in Etowah County, about thirty miles
northwest of Jacksonville. As a young woman Pearl taught Latin
in a rural school in Heflin. "Hell Fell In" she called the town. Her
imagination was stocked with Bullfinch's *Mythology* and the Norse
tales. The next layer was her family's history in the pivotal events
of the Revolutionary War and the Civil War. She was a member of
the Daughters of the American Revolution and the Daughters of
the Confederacy. She would sit close enough to me so that I could
smell her as if her odor was her voice calling me from a long way off
through the trees. As she told me this story, my grandmother would
fold her hands in her lap like they were two small animals asleep.

Sometime in April in the Shenandoah Valley of Virginia in 1863, my relation froze to death in a late spring snow. He was serving with the Army of Northern Virginia under General Lee. He was part of a regiment raised in western Georgia. He was a young man, married, with a boy and a girl back home on a small farm near Alabama. He was my grandmother's grandfather. All he had to eat were sweet potatoes roasted on the coals. But it was how he died that was the point of the story. To stay warm in the snow he had to lie perfectly still under a thin wool blanket. The snow would cover the blanket and act as a white quilt laid on top. But if he were to move, the snow would crack and the cold would be terrible. My grandmother's "papa" stirred and froze to death. The cracks in the snow were left as an unreadable epitaph to the dreams or the cramp that caused him to move. He was buried there under the frost-burned blossoms of apple trees and under another thin quilt. For a time his chest and thighs must have buzzed with activity, mirroring his own fantasies of home. My grandmother's hand would reach out and touch me to keep me still while she told the story. I couldn't tell if it was the dead grabbing me from underneath or my grandmother pulling me to the surface. In my living room now I have the mahogany and wicker-backed sofa and chairs that we sat in as she told me this story. The arms are black.

My grandmother was the family historian, chronicling the individual trajectories past lives left behind, though "paleontologist" might be more accurate, since the traces were usually left in paper or etched into a gravestone like a fossil. She was fastidious about her sources, which meant car trips to cemeteries. We drove south toward Horseshoe Bend, where Andrew Jackson had crushed the Creeks, to see a relation's grave. The church was small. The cemetery was sandy with patches of red clay. Plastic flowers in aluminum vases were turned over and scattered across the yard. My relation had been an Indian agent and married a Creek woman. Grandmother told me how he had been part of the negotiations around the exodus from Alabama to Oklahoma. The Creeks trusted him. He traveled with them to the new Indian Territory before abandoning his wife and coming back to his payoff. He was paid off in Creek land. No grass covered his grave. I chased a striped roadrunner lizard across the graves laid out like beds in a dormitory. The lizard was out of sight in an instant. I remember thinking I could track him. I looked carefully for the tiny footprints in the bare dirt. Before we left I went over to my relation's grave and spit on it. I told my grandmother and mother what I had done. That night in the back corridor of the big house I was sure that he was stalking me. I spoke to him out loud. "Forgive me," I said, lying. What I learned was how porous graves are. My spit could get to his face and he could get to me. The dirt was a curtain that could be pulled back. The moment I was floating on was like one of those underground rivers my grandmother told me about. The past seeps through to the surface, or a sinkhole could open up at midnight and a ghost could walk through. In my case it was a refrigerator.

When I opened the refrigerator door in the kitchen I could've sworn that I saw a swarm of black bees covering the tangerines, but it was just mold. I didn't know then that I was sick. Maybe it was the ghosts of my grandfather's hives. This had been the honey extracting room before the house was renovated. The bees were burned up when AC Jr. accidentally set the woods on fire trying to eradicate a bank of kudzu on the dam. The wooden hives and wax combs had fueled a firestorm roaring through a city of white towers. The bees zoomed in crazy zigzag patterns in the smoke. I singed my eyelashes and burned my face digging a firebreak through the trees.

Next to the tangerines the baloney was curled in a plastic sandwich bag. I found the bacon. I asked my wife, "How about a bacon, lettuce, and tomato sandwich?" "Yeah. Sure. Is there any mayonnaise?" The almost empty jar of Hellmann's was next to a piece of Tupperware stuck in the corner to catch a drip. I checked the expiration date on the yogurt. Just a few hours before the apocalypse the yogurt would become alive again. When I stuck my hand into some honey-like goo combed around the lettuce, I realized the refrigerator was a time machine. The bees were back.

There on the third shelf down, under the flour tortillas, was the fruitcake my grandmother Landers gave me the Christmas before she died. I was storing it like it was a brick from the walls of Troy. In the door was a jar of pickled herring in sour cream I had bought in case my dad ever came over. I'd even practiced what I would say. "Dad, would you like some herring with your beer?" Next to the Heinz ketchup was a jar of pickles sealed up tight in a powerful garlic gas; my grandmother Shelton had given me the jar for never painting the barn roof before it burned down. The refrigerator nicely preserves the wreckage. Next to the lettuce was a bouquet of red tulips with chocolate blooms on a dinner plate. The tulips were a Valentine's gift for my wife. I had a chocolate shop paint each flower head. I'd even checked to see if they could be eaten. The florist was very excited about the project, and as she spoke it was clear she was from Holland, making the purchase even more exotic. "Yes. The tulips are organic. No pesticides. They'll be delicious. The chocolate will taste a bit sweeter than regular milk chocolate." My wife was not excited. "They're weird." After that the tulips went into the refrigerator to slowly wilt except for their perfectly preserved chocolate heads that stare back at me.

The bouquet was a small catastrophe like the baloney or when I stubbed my toe on the bed going to get my three-year-old son a glass of water in the middle of the night. I talked to angels too. Benjamin doesn't give a name to the catastrophes that pile up around his angel. From his biography, it's not hard guessing the tragedies that gnawed at him. His personal grief was tied to the deteriorating situation in Europe before the war and the absence of a messianic moment in history that could have rescued him. For me, the messianic moment might be to unplug the refrigerator and send all the food to hell. In both of our accounts, though, there is nostalgia for the past and a desire to redeem it, preventing the horror the angel sees in the piling up of the wreckage. It all comes from somewhere. The holocaust is fed by pieces of biographies caught in the storm. My tulips were like a car wreck, preserved in the refrigerator, wrapped in crinkly green paper, the networks of exchange collapsed around them with a bit of red showing through a chocolate smudge.

"Ah, the lettuce is ruined. How about a bacon and tomato sandwich?"

"That's OK, I'm not really hungry anyway."

What would the tulips taste like, dabbed with mayonnaise on white bread with some crisp bacon? Like hell, I thought. In a passage completed in 1926 when he could only imagine how he would be engulfed by the wreckage at the end of his life, Benjamin writes:

> Cellar. We have long forgotten the ritual by which the house of our life was erected. But when it is under assault and enemy bombs are already taking their toll, what enervated, perverse antiquities do they not lay bare in the

foundations. What things were interred and sacrificed amid magical incantations, what horrible cabinet of curiosities lies there below, where the deepest shafts are reserved for what is most commonplace. In a night of despair
I dreamed I was with my first friend from my school-days (whom I had not
seen for decades and had scarcely ever remembered in that time), tempestu-
ously renewing our friendship and brotherhood. But when I awoke, it became clear that what despair had brought to light like a detonation was the
corpse of that boy, who had been immured as a warning: that whoever one
day lives here may in no respect resemble him.[1]

The passage portrays a set of encapsulated disasters like Russian
dolls in which one dimension collapses into another architectural
dimension, culminating first in what Benjamin calls "a cabinet of curiosities." But that is only the beginning. There is still more to come.
A dream of an old friend turns into a zombie warning Benjamin that
one day whoever lives here "may in no respect resemble him."

What for Benjamin was an unnamed cabinet of curiosities is for
me a Kenmore refrigerator from Sears, Roebuck I acquired when an
old woman in Gadsden died and her possessions were liquidated.
The Kenmore came out of the house with a dining room table with
big animal feet and a delicate four-post bed. They were all loaded
onto the back of a Chevy truck. There were no discernible marks
on the wooden furniture, and whatever magical incantations or
memories persisted in the refrigerator were wiped out with Clorox
spray. The pieces were like blank memory chips reset at my house,
or Frankenstein's brain turned back to zero. Nothing carried over
but the series imprint, Kenmore, which located me in a constellation
of kindred objects—Hellmann's, Tupperware, Hunter fans. Within
my cabinet is a cool world, a soft museum of decaying memories.
Even fruitcake has a life span. The cabinet of curiosity isn't a box

but a series of frames or sets that expands outward to the room, to the house, to the valley surrounding the house, and then contracts backward like the spiral on a snail's shell, back inside the Kenmore to the smaller cabinets, like the Dannon yogurt, which in turn opens out into a series of active ingredients that speed and creep into the person. In Benjamin's passage the supernatural figures strongly, but the uncanny is still drawn out of the human and not the ensemble of active ingredients. But what if spaces had their own architectural specters, or if objects like a refrigerator could act as a medium to the dead? Benjamin is already hinting at this with how mysteriously the cabinet of curiosity emerges in the passage as the heart of a network of architectural spaces. It beats like the heart in Poe's "Tell-Tale Heart." There in that configuration of herring, fruitcake, and wilting tulips I could have read the next fifteen years. It was all there like a hexagon from the *I Ching* or a scrambled message dictated from the Ouija board in the expiration dates, the stratified layers of relationships, the specific embodiments, the migratory patterns left by the fruitcake, the tortillas, and herring from distant worlds, and how my relationships were tied to objects like a floating red-and-white bobber, the hook embedded in my lip. The last thing my mother ate before her brain burst with an aneurysm was a bacon, lettuce, and tomato sandwich with mayonnaise. At the time I just couldn't see her there.

On the door of my refrigerator I have a note from my mother stuck on with magnetic strips from a café in Des Moines. I was in Iowa when the letter found me in a lonely exile from Alabama. The note read: "'A man who has been the undisputed favorite of his mother keeps for life the feeling of a conqueror, that confidence of success that often induces real success.' Life and Works of S. Freud." It was in an unmarked envelope with no return address.

No signature. I couldn't identify the author of the letter. For an instant I thought Freud must have sent it. He had found me in an obscure passage in an antiquarian work, recognized me as his descendant. Then in his will he arranged to have this letter sent posthumously. Or better, he dictated it through a Ouija board to a woman in Birmingham, where it was postmarked, and she sent the message, translating it into the shape of the only letter she knew how to write, a love letter. The shape of the handwriting and the postmark eventually gave my mother away. This is a kind of oedipalism Freud never imagined—the mother combined with the state. I called Mom on the phone to thank her. When I asked her why she hadn't signed the note, she said, "Why should I have? Who else could have sent it?" This was the second letter I had ever received from her. The first came when I was eight and lived with my grandparents in what I thought was a castle in Jacksonville, Alabama. My father was a Marine officer and had moved the family to an island off the North Carolina coast. I stayed behind in Alabama to finish the school year. I still have the letter I wrote back, which I found in a stack of papers after she died. The Freud letter was to be the very last one. My mother died a year later.

What did I expect, anyway? The tulips were like a paper cut across the grain of my finger that burst into bloom itself. Should my wife have eaten them one by one or put them in a vase on the kitchen table? If she had, there would have been a different wave of wreckage blowing into paradise. The fan might have dropped from the ceiling. The tulips were part of an exchange that materialized into a future I couldn't see then. Benjamin dedicates the book the passage above is taken from to a former lover: "This street is named Asja Lacis Street after her who as an engineer cut it through the author."

What Benjamin couldn't possibly guess at the time is just how prophetic the dedication was. A one-way street had him like an undertow, pulling him backward into disaster.

The tulips were the core of a tentative messianic moment in which the future could have been reinvented. The exchange wasn't limited to me. The hosts of heaven were involved. But it wasn't into the future I wanted to flower, to go, but to the past. I wanted to reinvent the past and send a flower back in time to the angel so that somehow the present could be reassembled. The Argentinean writer Jorge Luis Borges captures this paradox in his discussion of an unfinished novel by the American Henry James:

> In *The Sense of the Past* the nexus between the real and the imaginary (between present and past) is not a flower, as in the previous stories, but an eighteenth-century portrait that mysteriously represents the protagonist. Fascinated by this canvas, he succeeds in going back to the day when it was painted. Among the persons he meets, he finds, of course, the artist, who paints him with fear and aversion, having sensed something unusual and anomalous in those future features. James thus creates an incomparable regressus in infinitum when his hero Ralph Pendrel returns to the eighteenth-century because he's fascinated by an old portrait, but Pendrel needs to have returned to the eighteenth-century for that portrait to exist. The cause follows the effect, or the reason for the journey is a consequence of the journey.[2]

This is a familiar theme in Borges, the infinite regression. In Benjamin it was compulsion. In neither of our accounts does the angel have a name or the tulips a variety. They are forces. In 1932 Walter Benjamin began working on his most personal and arguably his most beautiful essay, *A Berlin Childhood around 1900*. The essay was never published in his lifetime. It was another one of Benjamin's defeats. Around the construction of this essay, Benjamin was being ripped apart by a succession of other defeats—his divorce, dwindling finances, the Nazis, a tragic love affair that pushed him toward his suicide. In the thick of these disasters Benjamin was quietly assembling a history of nineteenth-century Paris composed almost entirely of quotes. The quotes were laid like digital tiles into a mosaic that was designed to be reassembled into new patterns by the reader. This was a solid piece of holographic history. The essay on his childhood marked the break point in his larger project of facing the history of capitalism in the nineteenth century with his allegorical history of the moment of emergency in the twentieth century. His childhood becomes the foyer to the vast and arid disasters of this history. Benjamin was building a memory palace laid over a power plant. By placing his history in the nineteenth century, Benjamin chooses the world of his grandmothers for the center of gravity behind *The Arcades Project*. But it is a world in which their bodies have already largely vanished into the arrangement of furniture in a room or a certain configuration of objects on the table. An imperial grandmother is too large for a cabinet of curiosities. It is the urban wilderness that held his grandmothers like jewels or Madonnas that haunts him.

Benjamin had virtually no operating capital, no assistance or institutional support on a daily basis. He projected the investigation from his marrow and memories, sorting meticulously through volumes in the library for the suitable passages for his history. He was, as often pointed out, born under the sign of Saturn. I was given a chance to do my own Arcades project when my mother died. Shortly after the funeral, my father took me into a room dominated by a thick pine table fifteen feet long and three feet wide that had been made from a church pew. On it were stockpiles of books, papers, photographs, letters, and documents in avenues of columns that looked like a paper city. These pieces were all part of the genealogical project my mother had devoted herself to in assembling a history of the family. Before her my grandmother had collected the stories and overseen the genealogies. The ghosts that were part of this project were extra. My mother believed in the other world. She would matter-of-factly talk about seeing an Indian with a Mohawk lounging on the loveseat in the living room. He was her guardian angel. The very day she died she saw her dead mother sitting at the kitchen table playing a game of solitaire. She didn't say anything, just simply looked up and continued playing. "Allen, she was as real as you or me." She told me over the phone. "Mom, what was she wearing?" "She wasn't wearing a white gown, smarty-pants, just that robe she liked to wear in the morning." I wondered whether my grandmother could see the Indian with the Mohawk. That was the last time I spoke with my mother. My mother and grandmother loved bacon and tomato sandwiches.

My father wanted me to finish the project. He saw the history in military terms—organize, photocopy, bind, and distribute to each member of the family. I nodded a lot as he talked. "No problem. I can do it." Of course I was lying. I can't do it. The classic expression of this project in sociology is C. Wright Mills's formulation in the essay "The Promise." In a quick series of images he laid out the horizon: "Neither the life of an individual nor the history of a society can be understood without understanding both," and then

Nowadays men often feel that their private lives are a series of traps. They sense that within their everyday worlds, they cannot overcome their troubles, and in this feeling, they are often quite correct: What ordinary men are directly aware of and what they try to do are bounded by the private orbits in which they live; their visions and their powers are limited to the close-up scenes of job, family, neighborhood; in other milieux, they move vicariously and remain spectators. And the more aware they become, however vaguely, of ambitions and of threats, which transcend their immediate locales, the more trapped they seem to feel.

Underlying this sense of being trapped are seemingly impersonal changes in the very structure of continent-wide societies. The facts of contemporary history are also facts about the success and the failure of individual men and women. When a society is industrialized, a peasant becomes a worker; a feudal lord is liquidated or becomes a businessman. When classes rise or fall, a man is employed or unemployed; when the rate of investment goes up or down, a man takes new heart or goes broke. When wars happen, an insurance salesman becomes a rocket launcher; a store clerk, a radar man; a wife lives alone; a child grows up without a father.[3]

But Mills's description is a dry melodrama. Mysteries have risks, and they are messy rather than discreet. Everything is sticky and wet like a sweet fog. The relationship Mills conceives between biographies and the larger historical structures is more like a network of passageways running through houses and bodies and expands and squeezes spaces just like a vascular system. The individual is an interactive skeleton in motion, a prosthetic suit of images with passageways connected to the geography of the valley and those supernatural entities like the Indian with a Mohawk.

Even though both my father and I see this as a remembrance of my mother, this is never brought up, nor is the fact that the papers are cluttering up a perfectly good table. My father intends to clear the junk out. I see the project very differently. The papers are like strands of my mother's hair still attached to her head. Her hair keeps growing or moving inside the coffin just as if she were a new species of sleeping beauty four feet under the earth. It is an uncomfortable simile for me. The hair brings my mother's body into my hands. The project has my mother's weight. I wonder if I'll see the Indian stretched out on the loveseat in the living room or a swarm of black bees from those burned hives. In the early summer I found a migrating swarm in the pecan orchard hanging from a privet branch eight feet in the air. I set up the stepladder. Carefully cut the branch with a pair of loppers sprung against my chest for leverage with my right hand clutching the wooden handle while my left arm held what felt like ten pounds of bees on the thin branch. I carried the bees to the super, a box component to a hive with frames strung with beeswax. I brushed the bees gently with a horsehair brush into the box. Less than a week later, while cutting a swarm out of the privet, I yanked what I thought was a cut honeysuckle vine wrapped around a branch holding the bees. The swarm fell on my head like a water balloon. I was wearing a helmet and a veil and gloves, but no coveralls, just a thin shirt and jeans. It was like kicking a big blender on. Within minutes I had been stung hundreds of times. I ran back to the house with a cloud of bees shaped like a chainsaw cutting on my brain. My wife looked out the door. She was afraid of bees. She locked the door. My dog ran under the shed yelping. I stood there drenched in bees until there were no more. Peeling my clothes off in the kitchen showed me covered in a thin fuzz of stingers like a hair suit. Mom called. Her father had almost died after a bee accident. She wanted me to go to the hospital. My body parts had swollen to twice their size. I got sleepy. I dreamed about nothing that I can remember. The thick hair of bees that had been wrapped around me left me red and itchy. There is a picture of my mother, in which her hair is thick as bees.

Out of my mother's dead body a fog emerged that filled the lower reaches of the Barnwell pasture across from my house. The Black Angus stood still. The clouds slowly pulled through. What my mother saw as a single ghost with definable arms and legs and a specific hairstyle I saw in that momentary landscape as a single cow suddenly emerging from the mist looking at me sideways from one hundred yards away, a calf at her side. I wouldn't see a single ghost. I would be sunk into that landscape, which was disappearing into the fat air soaked with moisture. It was impossible for that cow to know my name. But the entire herd would come to me if I imitated my grandfather's yell. He would holler, "Come on. Come on." Suddenly I would be surrounded by thirty-three cows, a gigantic bull, and calves. Each animal was tagged with a number in the ear—it was a registered herd—each one watching me as intently as a haunting.

The German writer W. G. Sebald found such a fog lying on him in the hospital one late evening after surgery. He acknowledges the painkillers coursing through him and how pieces of conversations stalked out of the mist and sounded more like birds or sirens than two nurses gossiping. By morning, he is more aware. The talk is clear. Out of his window in the sky he sees the vapor trail left by a jet. "At the time I took that white trail for a good omen, but now, as I look back, I fear it marked the beginning of a fissure that has since riven my life. The aircraft at the tip of the trail was as invisible as the passengers inside it. The invisibility and intangibility of that which moves us remained an unfathomable mystery for Thomas Browne, too, who saw our world as no more than a shadow image of another one far beyond." Browne, it seems, in a note Sebald quotes just prior to his hospital description, does. Browne writes, "The great fog that shrouded large parts of England and Holland on the 27th of November 1674, it was the white mist that rises from within a body open presently after death, in which during our lifetime, so he adds, clouds our brain when asleep and dreaming."[4] Sebald never mentions directly the dead that cloud his head; two friends die in the very same chapter and hundreds of thousands in his descriptions of the air war over Germany and then the Belgian Congo. Inside the mist is what Walter Benjamin might have described paradoxically as "profane illumination." The fog doesn't obscure. It is the veil that separates worlds laid across the landscape. A year before her death my mother wrote in her diary, "Today I began the journey." At nearly midnight on Mother's Day, Mary Janie got up with a headache and then fell with a massive brain aneurysm. She never regained consciousness. On Wednesday morning, three days later, she was unhooked from life support and declared dead. Mary Janie was with her Mohawk angel on Mother's Day in the dreamworlds of Alabama. She was buried in the Jacksonville City Cemetery in the open sun next to her mother and father. There is an exposed water hydrant that sticks out of the grass nearby. The inscription on the marble stone reads simply "an uncommon lady."

After my mother died, my father moved to the top of a mountain. He is the second in a line of Sheltons in this valley. First there was AC, who moved east from the Black Belt as a young man, then AC Jr. the Marine captain, and then me, AC III. I'm not as tall as either my father or grandfather, and I am the last of the series. AC died the year before my son Tyree was born. My father's house is a small castle anchored to the rocks. Black bear and wild turkey occasionally wander into the parking lot, which is the size of a tennis court, cut into the hillside by the house. My father likes big parties. The view from the house is spectacular. The whole valley spotted with new houses can be seen before the view fades into the Talladega National Forest. The foreground of the view used to be my grandfather's cattle farm. He owned over a thousand acres in pasture and mountain land before it was sold off piece by piece. AC Jr.'s house is stuck on top of one of my grandfather's mountains. His house at night looks like a UFO hovering in the high sky. From his porch you can see the taillights of jets setting down in Atlanta ninety miles away. You can also pick out my old farmhouse, the line of longleaf pines that followed my property line, the beaver swamp, and at the far end of the pecan orchard—my ex-wife's new home. Dad has a mountain clouded with views back into memories.

Around the deck are feeders for small birds like the nuthatch. There are bluebird boxes in the clearings. My father has left tree trunks sawn off at eight feet for the woodpeckers in the surrounding woods. I can't help but think of the pecan tree framed in my kitchen window. Here these trunks look like coffins propped up for a photograph. Over the valley turkey vultures slowly circle on the updrafts. Dad has unexpectedly become a bird-watcher. A pair of binoculars and an Audubon field guide rest on the kitchen counter. My mother's mother fed birds and kept a big book of Alabama birds near the window. It could be that AC Jr. has always loved birds, and moving to the top of the mountain has made this relationship possible. Framed Audubon prints punctuate the walls. Images of eagles soar around the rock fireplace in the great room. I don't think my mother always saw angels and ghosts. She maintained that it was where we lived, not the house, that was haunted. Seeing the other world was only natural then. Angels infuriated my father. But there is an ancient tradition in which speaking in unknown tongues is described as the language of the birds. In his own way AC Jr. talked to the angels that surrounded my mother. I looked for her in the things stretched out before me. If the view from my father's house could be seen as an ensemble of sets arranged holographically, so that wooden structures like mule barns, houses, and feed troughs could be separated from the vinyl and aluminum structures, the newer Asian hybrids dotted round the newer homes could be shifted to different strata than those shrubs that arrived in the nineteenth century or the native species still holding on in the woods and in the recesses of the gardens, the grasses could be arranged in a time line based on their introduction into the valley, distinguishing Johnson grass from St. Augustine, or the tiniest imprint of lives left behind in the ground as scars and marks could be magnified for a moment, then something like the viewpoint of Benjamin's angel can be imagined. The angel sees not only the mounting wreckage of everyday life compressed into a rolling avalanche, but also the past stretched into a wide expanse in which everything is sinking, leaving historical structures like clapboard Baptist churches, and even species, like an arm sticking out of quicksand. My mother's passing into this world didn't stop the teeming dreamworld inside the fire ant mounds or cause a hive of yellow jackets to coalesce into a yellow bloom. Mary Janie was abducted into the future with barely a discernible trace.

The directions to my father's house on top of the mountain are straightforward. Turn at the rock entrance with the flagpole, then go straight up the drive for a quarter of a mile. The straight up part is what gets people. It's so steep that it's difficult to walk without leaning into a squatted crawl. My brother-in-law stalled a loaded U-Haul truck on the drive. The truck couldn't manage the incline without being unloaded into thirds. The driveway looks like a waterslide from a Las Vegas amusement park inside oakleaf hydrangea and scrub pines. AC Jr. treats the drive like the launching strip for a V-2 rocket. He guns his Jaguar up and down it, but he can't get county water that high. He has to pump his water up the mountain. His house on that mountain is the highest for miles, but it doesn't have a nickname. Across a cleft in the ridgeline, which drops down quickly to a dirt road called Crooked Mountain Road and then back up steeply, is Crooked Mountain itself. Crooked Mountain is small even by Alabama standards. Chimney Peak to the north-northwest is much taller and adorned with cable TV antennae and the remnants of an observation tower just four miles away. It is where it is, staring right down on AC's gone farm like a monstrous version of the madeleine in Proust. It has a name that only the old residents know. It doesn't appear on the map. There were no great views because of the pine canopy. It was just there like a big throbbing brain that was mute. My father has built an inclined moat around his house and this mountain. But this hides the most important facet of the drive. At the same time that the driveway was being constructed in segments, a solid marble block was laid on top of my mother's grave like a trapdoor to a subterranean temple. The driveway is a solid tear rolling down the face of the mountain or is the stem of an enormous flower laid in the ground for my mother. The drive is the centerpiece of the network of passages spread through the mountains that scribble her name in the forest. They're not part of the official network of county and state routes but something approaching a psychic system of unconscious passageways, forgotten roadways, abandoned and overgrown and then reengineered routes through the woods. The county road runs directly in front of AC Jr.'s house, linking State Highway 21 to the west with Highway 9 to the east. The original road in the mid-nineteenth century connecting the small community here to the nearest town, Jacksonville, ran through the mountains. This is officially named Forney Road after a rich local family's Confederate general. AC called the same road Crooked Mountain. The road ran helter-skelter through the mountains. It was wide enough for one fat car at a time clumping across potholes and rocks. Some sections were cherted, a flint-like rock composed of compressed sediment and organic compounds laid into the clay. On one side were the city dump and rats. On the other was Crooked Mountain, scattered with white refrigerators, piles of garbage, stacks of magazines, and rotting animal corpses seething with maggots. Now the road is officially closed. A pole gate is set in each entrance, but four-wheelers and four-wheel-drive vehicles have bypassed this obstruction by climbing around it and up the hillside.

As a girl my mother rode her horse over Crooked Mountain Road. Then the road was shaded by a canopy of longleaf pines. In the late 1940s and early 1950s these trees were decimated by pulpwood cutters. There are still some giant pines standing next to the road with no explanation as to why they were left behind. With most of the traffic choked off by the pole gates, Crooked Mountain is going wild again. Deer trails, which thread the sides of the mountain, drop down into the road more frequently. There are coyotes now. Near the top of the mountain a coon hunter built a monument to his dog. It's covered in graffiti. Somewhere else this would have been a shrine to the Virgin Mary anchored in flowering vines and rocks. The monument is a residue of a different religious order that is sinking slowly back into the woods. Together all these passages are part of a scriptural architecture that is shaped around a soft arcade. Like the cracks that formed over my relation's snow blanket,

these passageways are the exteriorization of a network of unconscious that is not just human but a hybrid—of my father, the four-
wheelers, the pulpwood cutters, the coyotes, the Creek Nation, the
fire ants, Crooked Mountain, the fruitcake, the refrigerator, the Indian angel with the Mohawk, the mattock—that has been cut into
the soft terrain laid over the mineralized structures of the mountain itself. In Benjamin's usage the glass and iron structures of the
arcades in nineteenth-century Paris acted as the hard framework
for the proliferation of the commodity as an active species and fos-
tered the emergence of what Max Weber might have described as
the "steel-shelled individual"[5]—rendered in Parsons's 1923 translation as "iron men"[6]—a person characterized by a smooth exoskeleton, a crustacean shell of integrated commodities; a coat, a
hat, iron pants, brogues cemented together. The haunting overcoat
Gogol wrote about in St. Petersburg in the 1830s emerges at the
end of the nineteenth century as not just a specter but a wereobject,
half human, half coat, and as hard as iron to penetrate. My relation's death in the Shenandoah Valley refigures Benjamin's hard
arcades into something softer—emphasizing the ephemeral, things
that rot, things that formed momentarily in the snow as an exter-
nalization of a hybrid unconscious that is only partially human laid
over a calcium, not iron, framework. Both Benjamin's and my own
usage read in these structural marks a form of scripture stood up
on legs. The passages are part of a capillary system that holds my
father and my mother as tightly as anything Foucault envisioned in
his carceral system. But something is missing.

Borges notes that in the Qur'an there are no camels. The author,
Mohammed, had no need to include camels. He knew he could be
an Arab without them. On the other hand, the first thing a forger

or an Arab nationalist would do is fill the pages with caravans of camels swarming the desert. Their absence is one guarantee of the Qur'an's authenticity. Borges doesn't go on to mention that the trails and roads the camels traveled are likewise omitted in the Qur'an. If the passageways are there, they are thick with the ghosts of camels carrying the Qur'an on their backs in long endless caravans across the desert. That which is omitted in the network around my father's house is me running over Crooked Mountain hundreds of times, ostensibly training for marathons while trying to find the Indian with the Mohawk. I wanted to see what my mother saw in the cracks that broke over my relation's grave.

"To a consciousness that suspects it has been abandoned by human beings, objects are superior."[7] Adorno's comment was aimed at his mercurial colleague Siegfried Kracauer, but it could just as easily have been transposed to another member of the Frankfurt School, Walter Benjamin. Benjamin was fascinated by small things and their jewel-like shine and even more committed to the metaphysics of objects than his predecessor Kracauer. With Benjamin, Adorno's one-liner was expanded to a series of letters stridently criticizing his position, though tellingly, Adorno never pointed publicly at the erosion of human relationships around Benjamin. Perhaps he should have. As he neared the end of his life Benjamin was increasingly isolated geographically from what was left of his family and close friends. His exile in Paris accentuated Benjamin's experience of the great hydraulic achievement of the nineteenth century—the recession of humanness into pools and lakes at the heart of the commodity. Marx describes this process as commodity fetishism, but his interest is only tangentially related to the simultaneous destruction of one zone of wetlands and the formation of a new set of great underground lakes in the proliferation of the commodity. He more cautiously imagines a simultaneous expansion of the human in the commodity where his famous dancing table confronts a stationary and mesmerized individual trying to eat lunch. But both are human and alive. Benjamin was poised to take a more radical approach. New species of wereobjects, half human and part thing, were emerging in the hothouses of the arcades. Here Benjamin could just as easily have been describing the Galapagos shoreline:

> In the arcades, one comes upon types of collar studs for which we no longer know the corresponding collars and shirts. If a shoemaker's shop should be neighbor to a confectioner's, then his festoons of bootlaces will resemble rolls of licorice. Over stamps and letterboxes roll balls of string and of silk. Naked puppet bodies with bald heads wait for hairpieces and attire. Combs swim about, frog-green and coral-red, as in an aquarium; trumpets turn to conches, ocarinas to umbrella handles; and lying in the fixative pans from a photographer's darkroom is birdseed.[8]

One significant feature of Benjamin's passage is the absence of anything carnivorous or anything with the dread Freud consolidated in his usage of the uncanny, which is in the end based on how dolls stare back in such a way that scrambles the familiar and the homely into a wereworld. There is none of this dread in Benjamin's writing on toys or another zone of externalized humanness to which he devoted himself—books. Instead, Benjamin is an avid collector, an avocation that interjected itself into odd circumstances of his life. In his *Moscow Diary* Benjamin is attempting to rescue his floundering love affair with Asja Lacis and to solidify his commitment to the Soviet experiment in communism. Asja had suffered a nervous breakdown and was involved with another man. Stalin was tightening his control of the state. Both attractions end badly for Benjamin. The toys pop up around pathetic love scenes and disillusionment. The diary ends with this scene:

> I slipped away from her without giving her a tip, and made my way out of the hotel with Asja following me with Reich's coat under her arm. I asked her to hail a sleigh. As I was about to get in, having said goodbye to her one more time, I invited her to ride to the corner of Tverskaia with me. I dropped her off there, and as the sleigh was already pulling away, I once again drew her hand to my lips, right in the middle of the street. She stood there a long time, waving. I waved back from the sleigh. At first she seemed to turn around as she walked away, then I lost sight of her. Holding my large suitcase on my knees, I rode through the twilit streets to the station in tears.[9]

Benjamin was able to add new toys to his collection.

The fall before my mother died I had an accident. I was in intensive care for two weeks in a small hospital in western New York. My room was on the second floor, but I never looked out the window. I lay in bed with a thirteen-inch incision running from my groin up my abdomen. I had a tube stuck directly into my body collecting fluid. An IV drip and a morphine injector were hooked into my veins. The night nurse would pump me up with morphine as I begged her to stop. There was a cold burning sensation as it hit my blood. I dreamed in color for the first time. The nightmares were terrifying. In one dream I was speeding across surfaces and roaring into engulfing close-ups, what Benjamin would describe as the optical unconscious, the world that exists just beyond the human eye frozen into view by the mechanical. The changes in color and texture in the dream made me feel like a cosmonaut cut loose in outer space. I didn't see my dead grandmothers or grandfathers. I saw what Benjamin's angel must have seen, an empty landscape oxidized into brilliant colors, stretched into nothing but wreckage without the hint of personal redemption. What would that mean here? If I could feel the angel's arm around my waist, or if a feather would drop from the outstretched wings in front of my eyes, that would be redemption enough. In Benjamin's passage no feather drops from the angel's wings. There is no miracle. Instead, I, the tulips, the fruitcake, and the refrigerator were flying. In a line taken from another of Benjamin's essays, Walter writes, "I see, I fly." What Benjamin found exhilarating left me a solid nauseous block at the top of the Tower of Babel. I can feel an arm wrenching me loose with no certainty that it was God and not the night nurse.

I recovered alone in a cabin by a lake. I sat looking north into the water and sky with a blanket around my legs, rocking mechanically back and forth. My intestines were poking at the tender parts of my stomach like a snake trying to escape a cage. My mother and sister came the first day I was back from the hospital. They stayed a week. I didn't realize then that my mother was dying. I still have the instant coffee she bought in my cabinet and an unopened package of vitamin E soap. Nor did I understand that this scar was another passageway in the network around Crooked Mountain. It would be a cesarean scar that brought my mother to me before her death. This was the angel's feather. She died in Alabama, while I was asleep in the Finger Lakes. Within a month I would be back in a hospital for surgery. There would be another surgery a year later. The effect was to deepen the color of the scar and the certainty that this line across my abdomen would lead me like the cracks in the snow to the arms of the dead.

Just before his death at the French–Spanish border, Benjamin was described by his companions on the trek across the mountains as lugging a heavy black briefcase that contained what Benjamin reportedly said was "the most important thing to me. I cannot risk losing it. It is the manuscript that must be saved. It is more important than I am." Detained at the border, Benjamin took an overdose of morphine. The briefcase was never recovered, and its contents remain a mystery. If only that briefcase had been a person holding his hand. Benjamin was not particularly physically fit, and the climb exhausted him. Here is where Benjamin needed to be clutched by an angel. His last bit of energy seems to have been expended on that briefcase. What it contained has been the object of intense speculation. But the image of Walter Benjamin as a Santa Claus dressed in a black suit and lugging that briefcase under the September sun sharpens the irony of his death. After his death, the party was allowed to cross the border under the sign of Benjamin's farewell valentine. The surrealist Georges Bataille thought that Benjamin was carrying a version of his history of nineteenth-century Paris written as a children's story. In it toys, combs, bodices, pocketknives haunt the passageways through the city and move about while the city sleeps. Against this enchanted sky an autobiography of Benjamin appears in the unnamed narrator, who as he goes to sleep says goodnight to the objects that become alive as he falls asleep. Goodnight briefcase. Goodnight manuscript. Goodnight mustache comb. Goodnight doll. Goodnight ink bottle. Goodnight map of Manhattan. Goodnight postcards. Goodnight toothbrush. Goodnight brogues. Until finally in the twilight moment in which he is half asleep and they are half awake, he says his last incantation. Goodnight Moon.

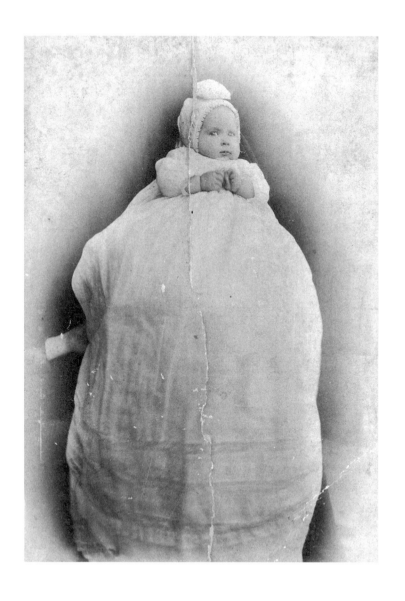

Planchette, My Love

A commodity appears at first sight an extremely obvious, trivial thing. Its analysis brings out that it is a very strange thing, abounding in metaphysical subtleties and theological niceties.

— Karl Marx, *Capital*

Deer hunters found what was left of Smithy's body sucked into the gray mud at the edge of a lake on the top of Cheaha Mountain. The body was hidden away like a forgotten Christmas present in the bulrushes. Smithy was now part of the lake at the highest elevation in Alabama and moved imperceptibly with the subtle currents. Smithy suddenly had grace and a moral density he could never have imagined. The flannel shirt and the Plain Pocket jeans he was wearing were almost translucent. His feet were bare. Whatever he had in his pockets was gone. He used to carry a big pocketknife and a wad of keys on a strap connected to his belt. I think the knife was an Uncle Henry with a bone handle. It had been a year since he had disappeared. His pit bull had starved to death on his chain before anyone realized he was gone. Smithy lived alone on a small farm littered with the ruins of wrecked tractors and ramshackle outbuildings. He had never married. He didn't have any friends. He had killed old man Snyder in the road with a shotgun as he was bearing down on him in a three-quarter-ton Ford. They had been feuding for years over their property line. Smithy's corpse was a good forty miles from home, the longest trip he had taken in years.

Smithy had dug the spillway out of the Big Lake on my grandfather's farm. It wasn't a graceful cut. Smithy plowed a ravine for a hundred and thirty-five yards through the growth of sweet gums, water oaks, and tulip poplars. The sides were cut straight up and down. Tree roots curled out into the air seven feet above the muck like arms grabbing for a hand. From the top of Crooked Mountain a mile and a half away the ravine looked like a moccasin snake's carcass strung through the trees. The mountain itself was a snake, a piece of Rattlesnake Mountain that reached south toward the flatlands and north toward the Appalachians.

The valley around my grandfather's farm was a network of ruins—teetering wooden houses, graves falling into shallow yawns in the ground, dilapidated barns—overlaid with brightly colored houses and trailers on green, scraggly lawns.[1] What had been small cattle farms and tiny cornfields were turning into residential properties. Smithy's house was a rough-cut box cobbled together out of exposed insulation, sheets of fiberglass, and asphalt shingles. He and his shotgun were out of sync with the air conditioners, vinyl siding, and higher property values. But there were other notable features in the landscape. Scattered through the valley were long aluminum chicken houses that floated like moored dirigibles in the full sun, each spreading the smell of chicken shit for three-quarters of a mile in all directions. On the dirt road that wound through Crooked Mountain were piles of garbage mixed with refrigerators, melting horses, and cows with beetles swarming over their guts next to stands of deciduous azaleas and oakleaf hydrangeas. Objects, flora and fauna, and practices from different worlds were jammed together in aboveground geological patterns. In the sixties one of the buses in the Freedom Ride from Washington, D.C., was burned on Highway 78 nine miles down the road. A man was killed. Just north was an old lynching zone from the early 1900s that had turned into the center for drug trafficking in the state. Two FBI informants had been murdered there by the redneck Mafia. Michael Taussig, an anthropologist who worked on the violent remnants of the rubber trade in Colombia, would describe the valley around my grandfather's farm as a part of a "culture of terror, a space of death."[2] For Taussig, landscapes can soak up stories and practices and then ingest individuals in a whirlpool of sticky signifiers, coating the person in a prosthetic as natural as a baby's skin and as complete as anything the German sociologist Max Weber imagined with the "iron cage."[3] What neither Weber nor Taussig directly articulates is the coordination between body and the surrounding landscapes. The fit or coordination is more than an ecological adaptation. It is radicalized habitus in which the two landscapes are sewn together by the same "set of needles."

It's not just a metaphor that ties Smithy to the ravine but a net of intertissular meshworks. The scar on his left forearm looks like it could have been from barbed wire ripping back under tension. I have a small one in the same place. The ravine is a larger scar. From Crooked Mountain this is exactly what it is, a rip gored through the humus and red clay by a backhoe under hydraulic pressure. Manuel

De Landa more eloquently describes this likeness as a consequence of common physical processes applied to landscapes at different levels, such as Smithy's body and the grove behind the lake.[4] De Landa moves toward abstract engineering diagrams to explain the similarity. Another solution is to see both scars as a consequence of establishing an ordered grid on the two landscapes. The world pumping in between Smithy, the tractor, my grandfather, and their minds merges into a ghost that finds expression in scars.

Crooked Mountain is a zone where ghosts and trivial events combine into layers of hauntings that reach through the landscape and bite, then vanish back through the thin topsoil into the red clay. Here the cunning of imprisoned rattlesnakes turns people like Smithy into pink meat for crayfish at the water's edge, a baby Moses for insects and birds in the bulrushes. The kind of space found in Colombia flexes between charged supernatural landscapes such as the Indian body, the jaguar, whiteness, the commodity in one of its most surreal forms: the hallucinogenic root *yage,* and the biggest of them all—the rain forest itself. The horror of the Alabama woods is different. The extremes are muted and are as elusive as the pileated woodpecker, a crow-sized woodpecker killed for its feathers, whose traditional habitat is vanishing with the clear-cutting of the old longleaf pines.[5] Here economic fictions bend and torque with the religious in a matter-of-factness that masquerades as normal business. Smithy dug the ditch my grandfather wanted for so much per hour. The straight business arrangement beguiles how intertwined, like honeysuckle around a sapling, Smithy and my grandfather's dreams and nightmares were with the project of domesticating wildness through hard work and how hidden their own characters were in the digging.

Smithy didn't go to church. The only time he ever mentioned God was next to the idea of killing those Japanese sons of bitches. He worked hard. His tractors looked like shit but they ran. The tractors, like the rattlesnakes he baked in his toolbox in the August sun, were instruments of his will dedicated to accumulation and not preservation. Smithy didn't accumulate objects but a singular view of himself as a compounding bank account. His body double was found in the netherworld of banks, a thing made of interest and paper bills. This paper statue of himself mesmerized Smithy. No Madonnas in the woods or bloody Christs moved him. Smithy was the embodiment of a new saint. He smelled like diesel fuel. He was murderous. But his prosthetic covering was as smooth as any saint's marble or as glossy as Gregor Samsa's shiny black shell. What Smithy did is make true the retrofitting of Weber's iron cage into a steel or titanium coating indistinguishable from the person's character.[6] Smithy had $70,000 in his pocket the night he disappeared.

Crooked Mountain was like a big throbbing brain at the center of the landscape. It was the biggest ruin, the biggest grave, and the gravity that moved toolboxes, pine beetles, deer, sofas, hope chests, and packs of wild dogs across the landscape. From the top of Crooked Mountain, the whole valley could be seen. Smithy's farm was north across Turner's hog farm and the rock quarry. From the mountain it was indistinguishable from other farms, just another open field temporarily rescued from the pine trees and broom straw, the first stage in a succession of plants and men who lived there and the whacked pH of the soil.[7] Fields covered in broom straw, a stiff-bladed grass that can pierce the stomach of a cow, signal neglect. The pasture has been overgrazed without fertilization. The pH of

the soil is too alkaline and doesn't support better grazing grasses.
It is also indicative of an ecosystem restabilizing the conditions that
are favorable to an alternative and previous ecosystem—one more
suited to the zone than the artificial grazing pastures cleared from
swamps or pine woods.[8]

The spillway petered out in a stretch of dirt beneath an enormous tulip poplar tree. In May the tree is covered with bees and
fat blooms. The honey from a tulip poplar won't turn to sugar. I
never made any money selling honey, sugar or no sugar. Smithy disappeared owing me money for five gallons of honey. That came to
about thirty dollars. He thought the honey would help his arthritis.
"Goddamn Japs. Those little fuckers messed me up in the war," he
told me as he conned me out of the honey while rubbing his left
shoulder. Smithy hated anyone who drove a Japanese truck. "I'll
bushhog around the barn next week, Shelton. Soon as I get done
with Murray's septic line," he said as he eyed my Toyota one ton.
Smithy was last seen at a bar on Highway 78, an easy connection
to that lake at the highest altitude. Witnesses recall Smithy brag-
ging about how much money he had in his wallet. He had sold his
backhoe. He was going to Florida to party. Smithy was never very
smart. Some things are expected of a man who kept rattlesnakes in
his toolboxes.

His body and the landscape he dug were fitted together like a
set of holographic Rosetta stones laid against each other. Each was
covered in a pictographic language of scars and barely visible tracings laid into fat layers and humus. Together there was a repetitive
depth in which one small cut on Smithy extended into the larger cut
of the ravine with but the slightest modification of meaning. Each
is a trail cut by a trajectory of assemblages in movement. A molec-

ular cloud of particalized occurrences composed of pieces of objects and bodies drawn out of different strata of time and site had moved across Smithy like a Portuguese man-of-war with its long, delicate tentacles marking him and then through him into the landscape he dug. When Smithy took his cap off to wipe his brow, there was a red line left behind on his forehead, splitting his head into two colored halves like an egg cut in two with a straight razor. He wore the cap too tight. Smithy had been beaten and then shot in the head. The bullet was never recovered. But the Bic pen–sized line it gored through his skull could easily be seen by the deer hunters who found Smithy in the mud.

The water didn't flow through the spillway but gurgled down through the red-clay bottom in thick, colored transfusions. Mosquitoes prowled the shade. North of the hardwood growth was a concrete cabin that was used as the bee house to extract honey. A black dentist lived here in the Depression. He ran a hog farm. It failed. South was the beaver swamp my grandfather drained. At the time forty Black Angus cows and a bull grazed it. On the edge of the lower southeast quarter of the hardwood growth against the pasture were three small crab apple trees, a sign of a home site that the grass had swallowed up. The apples were inedible. What had been the county road ran through the center of the pasture, dividing it into two large pieces. The road was constructed in the 1840s between the small commercial town of Jacksonville and the farming community of White Plains. My grandfather said there had been a blacksmith shop near the creek. Sure enough, horseshoes would come up through the dirt. "Mule shoes," Granddad would say, correcting me. Then he would bend down and scrape the shoe out of the dirt and toss it toward the barn. He wasn't sentimental.

My grandfather A. C. Shelton had a history with mules. He was born into a poor farming family in the Black Belt. His grandmother was a full Choctaw, the only fact I know about his extended family. There were one brother and two sisters. They used a mule to plow on the place. He came to the eastern part of the state in the 1920s to work for the college. On the side he ran a small mule barn behind his house in the city. Mules were the only draft animal anyone used. No Belgians, no Morgans, or any other horse were used around Jacksonville. He sold mules until World War II, when tractors started to creep onto the small farms. AC never bought a tractor or used a horse on the cattle farm. He preferred to work the animals on foot. "Horses make them wild," he'd tell me plainly, without hesitation. At the time I never thought much about whether there was a difference between a mule shoe and a horseshoe. It was a crazy quirk like his antipathies toward ice water and pepper. Now I try to imagine how it must have felt for my grandfather to hold in his hands an object from his childhood. No more mules. No more of the men who lived around them. I never thought to ask him if he missed his Choctaw grandmother. In a long footnote in *Capital,* Karl Marx wrestles with the question of why mules were the dominant draft animal in the South. He could just as well have been trying to figure out why the mule became the shape of emotion, a beaten stoicism in so many poor men from that era.

In his *Seaboard Slave States,* Olmsted says, among other things, I am here shown tools that no man in his senses, with us, would allow a labourer, for whom he was paying wages, to be encumbered with; and excessive weight and clumsiness of which, I would judge, would make work at least ten per cent greater than with those ordinarily used with us. And I am assured that, with the careless and clumsy treatment they always must get from the slaves, anything lighter or less crude could not be furnished them with good economy, and that such tools as we constantly give our labourers and find our profit in giving them, would not last a day in a Virginia cornfield—much lighter and more free from stones though it be than ours. So, too, when I asked why mules are so universally substituted for horses on the farm, the first reason given, and confessedly the most conclusive one, is that horses are always soon foundered or crippled by them, while mules will bear cudgeling, or lose a meal or two now and then, and not be materially injured, and they do not take cold or get sick, if neglected or overworked. But I do not need to go further than to the window of the room in which I am writing to see at almost anytime, treatment of cattle that would insure the immediate discharge of the driver by almost any farmer owning them in the North.[9]

What Marx saw in the mule was a piece of the materialist infrastructure for the southern economy and then for a psychic economy inside the same materialist economy that organized the treatment of laborers, the ground, and emotions into a sticky, inseparable moon pie assemblage. One could say that my grandfather had the temperament of a mule. He did not often take cold or complain if neglected. He died like a mule in a nursing home. One week before he died, he cried in my arms. He tried to run away. I saw him shuffling toward the exit, the nurses shouting at me to stop him. I grabbed him in my arms, and we looked at each other. Despite the Alzheimer's, he knew me. "Please get me out of here, Allen." I stammered, "I love you, Granddad," as the nurses arrived.

On a hillside overlooking the road was the ruined foundation of a house. The ground had split the foundation into mounds of grass and rock. Around the site shards of broken plates appeared after a hard rain. The farmer who had owned this house had stepped into a cut of the hills, next to a creek, and shot himself in the mouth and out the back of his head with a shotgun. His wife walked in a circle around the house destroying the plates in a wide wavy circle. The ruins were bewitched, yet there were no ghosts. At this moment, there are three of us left who remember the story: my cousin, the daughter, and I. The daughter lives in California now. She and her mother left Alabama for good after her father's death. The daughter came back in the seventies to visit family. She stopped at the farm. I took her back to the spot where her father died. She had never been allowed to see it while her mother was alive.

I used to bring thirty heifers across this hillside every afternoon to the Back Barn to feed them crushed corn and cottonseed hulls. I carried a hickory stick and coddled them along in a special language my granddad taught me to herd heifers with. It was a drawn-out sucking sound—suuk, suuk, suuk. Bulls you worked differently. They were less crazy than the heifers. Push the heifers hard and they would rip through the barbed wire fences or snap a plank in half. They could knock the shit out of you. Once through the gap from the upper pasture, the heifers would run down the open hillside before pulling up at the barn and mooing loudly. But on this day the heifers were stopped in a black circle, pawing at the ground just below the suicide's house site. In the middle was a six-foot rattlesnake coiled up, thick as an arm. I stampeded the heifers. I was afraid one would get bit. They ran off kicking up their hind legs and bellowing. The snake and I looked at each other. I beat its head in with the hickory stick. The body writhed. With my boot on its head, I cut the rattle off. In my hand the body felt like my mother's velvet loveseat in the shape of an arm. There were thirteen rattles. I threw the carcass into the woods in the same direction as the suicide. I kept the rattles in my grandmother's hope chest.

The chest was the size of a whiskey barrel four feet long and about three feet tall. The back hinge on the left was broken. When the trunk was opened the lid clunked back and had to be propped up like an old woman with a broken hip and leaned against the wall. The chest was stuffed with small pieces and fragments. There was an arrowhead my grandmother had found on her property in Clay County. My father's dog tags from World War II, a toy knight, stickers for honey jars printed with my grandfather's name, my Social Security card, a letter from my mother, a tape of me preaching for the Full Gospel Business Men (an organization of charismatic businessmen), a high school report card, Christmas ribbon, the deed to my house, and stacks of snapshots and portraits I had inherited from my grandmother were all swirled together inside the trunk. The trunk worked like a sealed Egyptian wind tunnel. Inside, the pieces flew at incredible speeds against a wooden sky, assembling and disintegrating into paper doubles of me—a Tower of Babel put together without mortar or design.

At the peak of Crooked Mountain was a cross made from two pine trees nailed together. The top was cut off of a small tree, making the crosspiece and the post. A handful of twenty-penny nails were hammered into the intersection and it was cross-tied with a rope. You can see the cross driving in from Jacksonville. It wasn't large enough to stare down on you; it was there like a man standing in the clearing between trees waiting for something to happen. It was another reminder of a body stuffed in the ground. All through the mountains were pieces of bodies. State Police Colonel Dothard told me Satanists used these roads for their rituals. They would bury the initiates alive in shallow graves for baptisms. Colonel Dothard looked stern as he explained this to me. But he and I knew there were real graves littered through the mountains. A coon dog was buried with a memorial plaque along the dirt road. Near the paved road was a small graveyard dating back to 1900 covered in garbage. Colonel Dothard didn't know about the Indian burial ground dating to AD 1 at the foot of the mountain. The graves were mounds of large rock laid in careful pyramid-shaped piles and terrace walls. All of them were now hidden in the recess of a succession forest.[10]

A surveyor laying out roads around my father's property stumbled onto the graves. What he saw were walls, not graves, and the pyramids he read as a farmer clearing a field. The graves were on a small hillside that gently rose at the bottom of the mountain near a spring before folding back into the longer slope of the mountain. My father told me I could build a house here. This would be my inheritance. But that was before the graves were found. The archaeologist from the local college, Harry Holstein, is set to begin excavation. He's waiting for the leaves to fall completely from the oaks and sweet gums in late January. Then the strategic digging will begin. In the interval my father found one large handmade brick beneath the leaf litter, confirming that the surveyor was partially right. There had been a farmhouse there in the last century. My father has the brick on the mantle. The curious thing is the brick's singleness; where are all the other bricks that were part of the chimney? Are they in a stream turning and tumbling, headed deep in flight back to mud, bewitched by the graves?

It was just after Smithy disappeared that my grandfather decided to fill in the ditch. He was always worrying about a cow or a calf falling in. That is why I got permission to use the ravine as my personal landfill. I had just begun the restoration of what was called the Big House on the farm. The man and woman who lived in the house for thirty years, John and Opal Parker, had moved out. The well had gone dry. John Parker was used up. They moved a mile down the road into a prefabricated house set right off the road at the entrance to a cut through the mountains. Stands of mountain laurel spread up the cleft of the slope, hugging the shade. Parker would sit, arms hanging down by his side on the narrow porch, wearing overalls and a T-shirt, and stare straight ahead at the passing cars. The general store at Rabbittown was a minute away at forty-five miles an hour, so there was always a truck or a Chevy whipping by. Parker had no money other than what Opal brought in. She worked at the chicken plant. Parker didn't go to church or watch TV. He couldn't read. He knew Smithy. He had seen Smithy dig the ravine. He thought Smithy got what he deserved. "Son of a bitch," he said. "Couldn't even dig a goddamn ditch right."

The Big House was partially sheathed in an exoskeleton of asphalt shingles added in the 1940s. The inside walls were covered in newspapers and a paint that was made from buttermilk. The walls were soaked in a baby blue color. Each room was identical in color. Beneath this newer layer was an extensive range of deep, lovely colors—sea blue, forest green, burgundy—and each door was false grained to resemble rich cherry woods. To get at these colors either lye and vinegar or large amounts of ammonia had to be applied. The ammonia had to be smeared across the buttermilk paint, which dissolved into a light buttery cream on the rag. Beneath these layers were the hand-planed pine boards with their watery grain running in long, wavy lines. It did not take much convincing to push me to expose the wood grain. Seeing the raw wood face emerge was purifying. It was not historically accurate. The vibrant colors were right. But the bare pine was wood without original sin. The lye turned the wood surface into a furry grain and had to be applied with a scrub brush alternated with buckets of vinegar splashed on to quench the chewing action of the lye. The ammonia was the best solution. I bought ten gallons of pure ammonia, an Army surplus gas mask, a mop, and a bucket. The ammonia created an atmosphere like the surface of Jupiter. It drove me to the windows gasping for air. The gas mask allowed me to go in the room like a diver with a limited amount of air time. Within three minutes the mask was pumping ammonia into my mouth. After three days spent stripping one room I gave up. My lungs were seared.[11]

The floors were sealed in layers of linoleum. Pulling it up was like peeling long strips of skin as the nails ripped and popped. Underneath were heart pine boards ten inches wide. On the stairs were maybe a hundred Mason jars packed with cloudy hunks of squash and beans that stared back like freak fetuses at the carnival. Dried animal tails hung from a string stretched across the room upstairs. Piles of clothes turned inside out after an orgy lay in clumps, half in and half out of sagging cardboard boxes. There were wooden boxes filled with spent rifle shells. Sprung steel traps were scattered across the room in a failed attempt to snag Santa Claus. A dead possum posed like the mummy of a pharaoh near the fireplace. Wasp nests, stacks of paper, an occasional snapshot, pop bottles, leather shoes flattened into shims whimpering to be touched again covered the floor. A wood-handled broom, the head curled into a swoosh, stood propped next to hundreds of wire hangers. There wasn't a closet in the house. Then there was the layer of mouse droppings;

the last stratum before the hand-planed pine boards. Parker would die soon. Opal and her daughter Rachel would visit and marvel at the deep color of the polyurethaned floors.

What they saw in the color of the floor was never mentioned. Maybe nothing, other than the kind of wonderment that they had lived for thirty years on top of these boards and had never known them for what they were. In the bedroom upstairs where Rachel had slept, she had written in crayon across the wooden frame door "Princess room." Now for a brief period, with the house stripped, the floors sanded and coated, it was an expanse of mirrors waiting for a princess. Opal is now dead for ten years. I've not seen or heard from Rachel in nearly thirteen years. The floors have lost their luster and a whole new set of objects is arranged in crowded constellations across the floor. I have been pushed out of the house, but my books, furniture, pictures, and even some clothes still prowl the rooms. In Georges Perec's novel *Life: A User's Manual,* objects are given a dignity as signs, residues of their previous owners. In the long, detailed inventories of active rooms where an individual still resides and in rooms where only pieces and debris persist like the Big House at the beginning of the excavation, Perec finds the hint of a larger meaning, almost a conspiracy of objects, whose cunning overwhelms the individual's intelligence. In *Capital* Marx writes, "Could commodities themselves speak, they would say: in the eyes of each other we are nothing but exchange values."[12] The floor spoke to Rachel even if it were at the level of the uncanny. In Perec, the uncanny exerts a constant pressure on the surface stretched between disparate objects, threatening to turn ventriloquism inside out and let the objects speak for themselves. My ex-wife painted over "Princess." The priest who blessed our bed ignored the 22-caliber rifle slung over the bedpost, the Jerusalem Bible by the bed, and the notes left on the wall by Rachel and a boy from 1917.

I backed the pickup truck slap against the back door. I'd taken a crowbar to the three steps reaching up to the door and crunched them off the house. The insides were tossed into the bed of the truck. The glass jars were laid carefully on top so as not to break them. Five loads were driven to the ravine and dumped. Empty, the house seemed delicate. Outside were snags of cranky tin sheets, splintered clapboard, and broken windows. These were piled into the bed of the truck in heaps. My grandfather stood to the side with his hands folded around his walking stick, the top button of his shirt firmly fastened and the sleeves drawn down his long arms. The outhouses stood like two hunched cathedrals over hard ground. I knocked them down with a sledgehammer. It was like clunking priests on the head. Shredded tires, rusty box springs, steel traps, shoes, broken hoe handles, car bumpers, crazy tangles of barbed wire wound into hair knots, and contorted aluminum chairs lingered inches beneath the dirt waiting for a giant magnet to pull them into a wave that could smother an angel. Without a magnet, I had to reach into the dirt. The dirt was soft as a belly stuffed with rotting compost. Big creamy grubs slept in the creases and wriggled like amputated thumbs once I yanked them into the light. Add to this the stuff drawn from a smaller, more personal radius of objects that held the smell of my body—a crashed vacuum cleaner, a murky-colored blender, aluminum pots and pans—and the ditch ached under the vertigo of swirling debris settling into the muck.

Into this vortex was dumped one particular object—my mother's Ouija board. She got it when she was twelve. World War II was pumping men in and out of the area. There was a large army base seven miles down the road. The Ouija board was wooden. Wood apparently is a better conductor of spirits. The board had lived in the attic stairway with my dead grandfather's books stacked around it blocking access to the top. My grandmother gave me the board as a keepsake.

My wife was terrified of that board. She had seen the movie *The Exorcist.* "That's how the girl became possessed," she would tell me. "The demon entered her through the Ouija board sheet she owned." The sermons at Faith Temple pushed this fear. The board was not just a passageway into the spirit world but an active agent itself that could move on its own across a room or cry out in pain. Claire Arnold, a mother of three teenage daughters, testified that when she burned a Ouija board in a pile of garbage behind her house, the board screamed in anguish. Peggy, a woman in her thirties, told how the planchette,[13] the heart-shaped mobile piece that traces the letters on the board, flew across the room, attacking her after spelling out how it would kill her boyfriend, "a good Christian man." These accounts circulated in the church. The preacher gave them credence. "These are end times. Satan is at work," he would intone. He told my wife to get rid of the board. The Ouija board was doomed.

To keep my wife in the house, I had to get rid of it. Because I would not burn it, she insisted that I bury it in the ravine with special precautions. It had to be at the bottom in the deepest section of the ditch. A wheelbarrow load of red clay went on top of the board. "Did you hear that? I told you it was haunted." She heard the sloshing sounds of the clay hitting the muck and the board slipping like a snake into the leaves. Then an ancient dingy steel sink and the wooden cupboard it sat in were thrown on top to ground the conductivity of the board. A plywood dresser was ripped apart and thrown in layers like quilts over a cold body. Then more clay was shoveled in the ditch, followed by a face cord of rotten firewood and pecan branches. The weight reassured her that the board would not wander home like a mangy dog in heat or slip out in the night like a thin wooden vampire. The weight was a stake in its heart. "Is that all of it?" she asked. She meant, had I thrown in the planchette, the spelling part of the Ouija system. "I threw it first," I told her. I loved my wife and yet I lied. I had hidden it in the deepest part of my grandmother's huge trunk in the study. Perversely, I placed piles of photographs of my dead ancestors around it. Perhaps this small act of infidelity is what eventually unraveled our marriage. The onus isn't entirely on me. My wife could never understand how artifacts from my mother's life were crucial in holding her to me. Others from Faith Temple would have more astutely pointed out how the planchette opened up a line to demons that would pull me into possession. If only they had known my secret. This would be the devil inside me.

I was already practicing possession, feeling the effects of the planchette whenever I closed my eyes to pray. I was at a prayer meeting in the parish hall of St. Luke's Episcopal Church. The church was two blocks from my grandmother Mary Pullen Shelton's house and next to the police station. This is a time that the Holy Ghost spoke to me. The form of the communication is called a word of knowledge. It wasn't dramatic. The message was part of a daydream while I was sitting in a tight little circle in folding chairs. There were nine of us. There were the priest and his wife. He liked to be called Father Joe. Next to Joe was my wife. Fain Edwards[14] and his third wife, Kay, were on her other side. They had been high school sweethearts. A year later, Fain, who was built like a round, muscular plug, would haul her off to Mississippi to have demons cast out of her. Rounding out the circle was a middle-aged woman who had a crush on the priest—they hugged a lot—and an old couple who had recently found Jesus at a retreat in Florida. We were praying and holding hands without interlocking the fingers, just palms. Fain and Kay were speaking in tongues.[15] Everyone else was quiet. I was sitting, half asleep, daydreaming. Above us was a portrait of a young child, an eight-year-old boy dressed in shorts and a bow tie. His family politely owned the town. He died shortly after the portrait was painted. The parish hall was dedicated to his memory. Kay picked up her cooing. She sounded pained. Did she already know she was going to Mississippi? It was around that sound that the Holy Ghost seeped into my daydream. I saw my life as a stack of uncaptioned photographs floating in a large trunk filled with ribbons, old deeds, and toys. There were no names on the photographs. The trunk was exactly like the one I had in my study filled with the old photographs my grandmother Pearl Baskin Landers had given me. In the crowd of people I could only identify my grandmother and grandfather. Everyone else was anonymous. In fifty years I would be just like these photographs, a face without an identity staring up out of the trunk. I felt an intense loneliness draining through me like a tide going out. It would've been far worse without that sense of movement. To be still like a photograph was to be held in a whirlpool, to be falling in place, to be turning like a screw in a swoon. The core of this feeling is an intense craving for what Freud described as the oceanic. What didn't materialize was the planchette. The planchette was unseen in the trunk, like a queen bee in a hive underneath teeming bodies.

A Love Letter From God

Dearly Beloved,

Let us share with you our vision for 1982 and ask you to be in godly agreement with us. For ten years God has continually stirred the desire in our hearts to be part of an end-time Charismatic Teaching Center. (If the vision should tarry wait for it; because it will surely come—paraphrased of Hab. 2:3). We desire to see this teaching center become a reality in 1982 for the perfecting of the saints, the work of the ministry, and the edifying of the body of Christ, until we come into the unity of the faith and the knowledge of the Son of God, unto a perfect man! (paraphrased from Eph. 4:11–13).
Love Clarice

Publications No. 10 Fluid Ministries January 1982[16]

On August 14, 1982, at approximately 7:37 in the evening, four men led by Fain Edwards came to the back of the church where I was sitting quietly taking notes on the service.[17] I saw them slowly materialize around Edwards as if he were magnetically charged—no words were spoken—and then stroll down the aisle of folding chairs. There were no pews. Edwards slipped into the aisle where I was sitting. I stood up placing my brown notebook and pen on the seat of the metal chair. My black leather Bible was placed discreetly over the writing. Edwards grabbed my arm. "The Lord wants to deal with you," he said. Edwards was a knife maker. He weighed two hundred forty pounds. Edwards was wearing an expensive English tweed jacket with leather elbow patches. He had a full black beard, very thick, no more than an inch off his face so he looked like he had two faces, one fitted inside the other. The other men were slight. They looked shrunken in their barely creased polyester cotton pants and white shirts. Their ties were clumsily tied and too short as if the ties were left over from childhood. It was remarkable how much they looked alike with sunken chests and skinny arms and legs and flaccid waists. Edwards smiled, showing a stack of teeth. "Praise the Lord, Allen." I said nothing, but looked around at the crowd waving their arms in the air like TV aerials and speaking in tongues. I started the walk to the front of the church.[18] At the front there were about twenty-seven individuals waiting in a softly undulating line. Behind me I could feel the pressure of two hundred people screwing a hole into my back. Attention was fixed on the prayer line. The line faced away from the congregation toward the band and the basketball goal, which hung from the ceiling. There was no altar. Instead there was a large fiberglass cross fastened to the metal wall. The church doubled as a gym. I wished I had stayed home and watched TV. I was deposited at the end of the line; Edwards and the four men went back to their seats. Only Edwards stood out in the crowd.

The church was a brand-new, gigantic, prefabricated metal building. The price tag was nearly $400,000 in 1982. It was paid for. The pastor's nickname was Smithy, just like the dead tractor guy.[19] He was a Pentecostal preacher who left his denomination to form his own church. He had been hugely successful. Starting off with a handful of members meeting in the funeral parlor, they soon moved into a renovated laundromat. After two years of this, the new church was built on the edge of town. Church services could run up to three hours. The congregation was poor, but one of the basic tenets of the church was the tithe. Money could be raised quickly. Fain Edwards was a dubious member of the upper end of town. His stepfather was a dean at the local college. Fain had gone through three marriages and a corresponding set of three fortunes. He was not liked in town, but he was part of the inner circle at Faith Temple. After his conversion to a born-again Christian, he threw his considerable muscle into getting everyone right with God. After his baptism in the Holy Ghost, he spoke in tongues that sounded like he was a Nazi SS officer barking orders, and he really started to piss people off. Me? What was I doing there? I was in graduate school in sociology. I was the guy who brought Fain to Christ. I had been going to Faith Temple for three years now. Everyone knew me. I even preached on occasion. I had friends there. I prayed with them, ate with them. I had gone on a church vacation with them to Florida. It was common practice to take notes during the service. Fain, however, suspected other reasons. He was wrong. It wasn't sociology. It was about discerning God's Word that had me there that night.

George and Clarice Fluid were preaching. They had come from Bastrop, Louisiana, in a zigzagging trajectory, hitting small interdenominational churches before coming to Faith Temple in Jacksonville, Alabama. Out in front of the church, their Winnebago sat like a big rottweiler. Their names and mission to do God's work were emblazoned on the side. Faith Temple squatted in the preacher's cow pasture. Fifty yards behind the church was a stringy barbed wire fence with metal posts teetering at odd angles, bent toward Jerusalem, Tokyo, Chicago, by the cows rubbing on them. Brahma crosses with white-faced Herefords grazed while whipping flies with their tails.[20] On the rise just to the northwest was the preacher's house, a cool, modern, split-level house. To the east was a small farming community turned into tract housing called Alexandria. The Klan used to be active here. The road to the north led straight to the old mill village built around the now dying cotton mill. Most of the congregation was drawn from here. They were called lintheads even though they didn't work at the mill. They just lived in the space that once was the mill's. The sins of the fathers are visited on their sons. The church was smack in front of the intersection, a big reminder that God worked wonders.

The church was stuffed with demons, tongue talkers, prophets in polyester, those who had come back from the dead, and Holy Ghost warriors.[21] This couldn't be seen from the outside. The parking lot looked just like the local used car lot or a building supply store on a Saturday. There were Chevy and Ford trucks, Jeep Cherokees, and late-model American sedans. Occasionally, Edwards would drive his Lincoln Continental to church. He had two. They were like identical twins in a mechanical reproduction of a steel and upholstered ménage à trois or an Adam and Eve at the end of time. The era of the American steel sedan was waning. My Toyota truck was the beginning of the new periodization of steel. By the end of the twentieth century, Japanese and Korean cars competed for the parking spaces. Inside the church, the textiles were quietly Asian. The made-in labels tucked behind the collar and the shoe tongue pointed toward a new shell for the body, a new kind of discipline exerting a pull toward China. Even Marx in the nineteenth century at the onset of the European capitalist expansion offhandedly acknowledged the haunting of China. In a footnote to his description of commodity, Marx writes, "One may recall that China and the tables began to dance when the rest of the world appeared to be standing still—*pour encourager les autres.*"[22] The French phrase means "to encourage the others," which is a reference to the simultaneous emergence in the 1850s of the Taiping revolt in China and the craze for spiritualism that swept over upper-class German society. The rest of the world was "standing still" in the period of reaction immediately after the defeat of the 1848 revolution.

I was at the end of the line. Clarice strolled down the line delicately pounding foreheads with the flat of her hands. She would rear up in front of the person standing perfectly still; her arm would shoot out like a boxer's right cross and spread like a starfish over the forehead of the individual. "Jesus. Praise God. Feel the power of the Holy Ghost," she intoned, alternating the phrases like they were part of a football cheer. It only took the slightest touch for the person to fall backward into clear space, arms folded or nailed to the side, back straight, into the arms of the man acting as Jesus catching the bride and in an act of romantic faith.[23] Clarice was a short, plump woman with a teased beehive hairdo. Her husband stood off to the side near the band in a black polyester suit. Everything was moving now except for those in suspended animation on the floor. One fifteen-year-old boy had chosen his position well. He was slain in the spirit next to a girl about his own age. While he was lying there, he would sneak a hand across and touch her thigh. She would unfold her arms, slap his hand, and refold into the saint's pose.

When Clarice got to me, the line was lying serenely on the floor.[24] She raised her arms to single me out. The congregation behind me was in pandemonium. The congregation looked like an anthill knocked over. Body parts were swarming to get to the queen. Arms, legs, and necks were squirming back into the shape of insects. She hit me three times and I wouldn't go down. I kept sticking my leg back whenever she would pop me on the forehead. After that she came in close and grabbed me around my waist. I was embarrassed because she had large breasts and she buried my face right in between them. She was wearing a strong gardenia perfume. She told me to take a deep breath and exhale. I breathed hard. She pulled me down and bear-hugged me, squeezing the air out. She then cast out a demon—the demon of unbelief.[25] She raised her arms again up over her head. There were sweat stains in the cleft of her shoulders. The church struck quiet as if someone had unplugged the amplifier. She raised her voice. "This man was Satan's. Now he is God's. I have cast the demon of unbelief out of him. He will be a great preacher. He will destroy the witches who bound him. Praise God. Praise you Jesus." She shifted her voice and moaned loudly. "This man will work great miracles in your name. He will heal the sick with the power of the Holy Ghost." She then laid her hands on my head, raised her voice over the congregation and anointed me with the Spirit, "I give you the power of healing. Praise the Lord." The congregation surged up into the air. Their arms fluttered and swayed as if a wind were blowing through the gym. My arms would barely move as I walked back to my seat. My Bible had been knocked to the floor. My notes stared back at me.

Clarice was able to effect the transformation with a sleight of hand. My refusal to fall down called the machinery into question. As she reminded the congregation, her voice booming over the waving arms and upturned faces, "Whoever I touch feels the power of God." This cue in place, it made it easy to act out the script. Each body on the floor was a cue card. I stopped the mechanical drama momentarily. Clarice was able to ad-lib a solution with a brilliant move. She reinvented the stop. I was demon-possessed. After the exorcism she recited my spiritual biography, slipping a new narrative discourse into how the congregation saw me. I was hunted by witches who wanted to kill me. I was the object of covens. I was followed by eyes that collapsed around me like wet sand. While I was a whole entity, a discrete individual like a surveyed plot of land with iron stakes at each corner, around me were packs, multiplicities, witches, eyes, covens, everything in the plural. The threat to me was a disintegration.

Clarice conjures up the same imagery. I was hunted by pieces speeding around me, cartoon horror with hyperanimation crisscrossing through me like razor-sharp eyeballs in a Looney Tunes cartoon. Clarice grabs hold of the individual, hands spread across the forehead, and then with her enveloping history remakes the person into a block. The congregation swarming like maggots in stigmata is only a temporary stage of movement and indeterminacy. It is headed for the block, the psychic foundation of capital, a castle straight out of Kafka. The saved sinner, one soul, the tithe are part of this stabilization into an architecture of the individual pinned in place. Clarice moved me from one person to another without ever allowing disintegration. The closest I came was the moment at which I was two. The demon and I were in a crowded house. She flicked through me as if I were a series of channels. She locked the remote down on channel 5. At the very end she did an ad for my transformation. "He [referring to me, she never got my name] now has the gift of healing. He will be a powerful voice for the Lord." With another couple of endorsements, maybe I could have been somebody.

What happened to me is not new. It is not uniquely postmodern. The politics of identity are at least as old as the sixteenth century in certain regions of Western Europe. Natalie Davis's[26] reconstruction of a sixteenth-century French village and the trial of one of its citizens (and that is the key word), Martin Guerre, points out that ambiguities around the self are not new. The Martin Guerre story is about who and how many pieces can occupy the same space. The trial centered on establishing if Martin Guerre was Martin Guerre. There were conflicting testimonies, conflicting evidence. The court and the village eventually define a Martin Guerre but not before implicitly defining the person as a performance within a structural network of relationships, property, and the growing French state. The self is an artifact of disciplinary apparatus, a fixing of the possible contingencies within a defined scene. To use the same terminology as I did in describing my interaction with Clarice, it is a block, a constellation of experiential capital with definable boundaries.

The contemporary politics around the self are connected to the speed and ease with which simulations proliferate in the new mimetic technologies. In Martin Guerre's world the mimetic devices are located in the memories of the neighbors, the shoemaker's pattern, the signature. The simulations are not only slower but more easily disciplined. The self and the scenes can be authorized. Clarice's problem is more profound. The televisual speeds things up. The single demon device is an attempt to slow others and me down into a block. Ironically, the televisual infuses her performance. She moves unself-consciously across the front of the church like a TV evangelist.

That the body is a battleground is axiomatic to Clarice and those at church who organize their arms, eyes, hands, and butts into embodied testimonies of their faith. The ecstasy of the spirits, the power of the Holy Ghost, doesn't contort the body. There are no spasms. Any spit is incidental. The women slain in the spirit lie on the floor with their arms folded like sleeping saints or saints being folded up for a UPS shipment. Their dresses are discreet. The Holy Ghost never blows them up around their thighs, however much of a Madonna Marilyn Monroe may be, floating through the netherworld of TV and the imagination. It is a disciplined wildness, a perfection of wildness through domestication.

Ringing the body of the saint or the possessed are systems of objects, gestures, and sentiments that function as a copy of the individual, the body being just a point of intersection at which the flows can be disciplined and articulated. Dan Rose describes these flows as active ingredients.[27] Like the tube of Head & Shoulders from which Rose pulls the phrase, the individual is a composite of ingredients temporarily articulated, temporarily held together as a block. The diagnosis of the person as either saint or possessed is a reading of the system surrounding the body as a nucleus or a focal point. It is an assessment of the possibilities and disciplines portrayed in the simulation.

I made an appointment to talk with Clarice about what happened the night before. I showed up in Levis and Nikes and an L. L. Bean button-down shirt. Outside in my truck was the new book, Hans Kung's *Why I Am a Christian,* I had special-ordered from the local Christian bookstore. The owner was perplexed. "Is he a Catholic?" Clarice was unavailable, still resting from last night. Instead, her husband George and the music leader, a woman in her midtwenties who was billed as an ex-Episcopalian, or Whiskapalian as she joked during her introduction to a set of cowboy Jesus songs, would meet with me. I met them in the preacher's recreation room. On the front porch, in oak swings and lawn chairs, the preacher, his deacons, and the Holy Roller big shots that could speak in tongues for sustained periods like multiple bursts from an M16 lolled around drinking sweet tea and talking God and football. Auburn would have a good team that year.

George spoke first. "How does the Lord want to deal with you?"

As he said it I realized how much it sounded like a chess move. Allen to king's bishop 5. George, firmly anchored by a rook and a crosscutting bishop, moves his queen to check. I was perplexed. How does one say, "I was the guy Clarice cast a demon out of, described in vivid detail how I was hunted down by witches, and then superblessed me with the gift of healing"? "Clarice prayed for me last night."

"Did you receive the gift of tongues?"[28]

"No."

"Do you speak in tongues?" the woman put in.

"Yes."

She continued, "Do you have a fluent prayer language?" That meant could I sound like an M16 raking a position across the field.

Like an Uzi, I thought. "Yes," I answered.

"What do you need?" Brother George oozed.

"I don't understand what happened last night."

"The Lord works in mysterious ways."

"I had a demon cast out of me."

"Praise God," they said in unison.

I knew it would disappoint them. "I don't think I had a demon." The room started to look like an emergency room. I was hemorrhaging. They moved toward me.

"Brother, let's pray." George and the woman surrounded me. George had his hands spread across my forehead. "What was the name of the demon?" He could have been asking the name of my cologne.

"Unbelief," I muttered. His hand squeezed tighter. The woman touched the top of my head with her fingertips. They both began to speak in tongues, which for all its mystery sounded remarkably like "I want a condominium. I want a condominium."[29] The process climaxed with George rearing back and pulling his hand off my head like he was ripping off a wig I had glued on a patch of bald skin.

"Spirit of unbelief, I command you to be gone."

"Praise God, bless you Jesus, bless you Jesus," the woman moaned.

I stood there perplexed. I felt nothing. This particular scene would be repeated two more times in the next forty-five minutes. In between, they would pray in tongues asking the Lord for discernment into the source of my demon.

"I see a record with a bloody ax on it," the woman said.

"No, no, don't have it."

"Oh, are you sure? You've never done drugs?"

"Never done drugs," I said.

"Never?"

It was clear they didn't believe me. I said "No," shrugged my shoulders, "sorry." They went back to rock and roll. "No, I don't have that album. No, I don't listen to them." Compounding the situation, I continually tried to argue that it was a cultural problem. All culture has fallen. Jesus is against the world, not just against rock and roll. It only convinced them more. George located the source of my possession in three areas. After one bursting prayer where both of them had squeezed my head pretty hard, the woman had a vision into my past. "I see an album cover with a man screaming on it."

I thought about it. I wanted to please them and reassure them that God still spoke to them. "That could be *The Court of the Crimson*

King by King Crimson. Great album." Like the television in *Poltergeist,* this was the conduit through which at least part of my demon came. The moment got even tenser when they found out I was a second-year graduate student in sociology.

"Sociology is the Devil's. You must burn all your books."

The final pipeline into me from hell was my furniture. "What kind of furniture do you have?" George asked.

I didn't hesitate to answer even as I thought that's exactly what I would ask. "Antiques, mostly primitive pieces, some old church pews my mother gave me."[30]

"Get rid of them. Go to Sears, Roebuck or Penney's. You're living in a house filled with demons."

I would not budge. I would not burn my books. I would not get rid of my furniture and get a new sofa from Sears. Paul himself quotes from pagan texts in his sermon in Athens. There is no indication anywhere in the New Testament for me to burn my books. Paul goes in the complete opposite direction, in fact. George and the woman stared at me. George shook his head and muttered "Jesus. Jesus." The woman seemed to be disappearing before my eyes behind George or into the very space where George was. She had shoulder-length brown hair, cut plainly and pulled back from her face. She was wearing knit slacks, a white blouse, and black, flat shoes. She had on a touch of makeup, especially lipstick, no eye shadow. She was slender, maybe five feet four, but was steadily shrinking into George. She held her hands in the air as if she were drowning. The one clue I had about her life before now was that she had been an Episcopalian. Maybe she had belonged to a country club with a domineering father who played golf, a mother who spent her time in clubs, and she had gone slightly bad before finding God.

"All truth is the Lord's," I said.

"Turn from Satan." As he said this George moved in front of the window in the room. He had on a blue blazer. It was polyester. The white shirt was opened at the collar. The collar was the size of a small bird's wings pinned to his throat. The way he smiled looked like a homecoming queen in drag. The middle button on the blazer dangled helplessly, stretched too often. Behind him, out the window in the preacher's pasture, the white-face cows were moving.

"What?" I said, snapping back to attention.

"Turn from Satan. Come back to Jesus." A cow looked in my direction. A sign? George rocked back and forth. The button jiggled at his waist.

"I am Jesus'." The woman was gone. She was swallowed up.

"You're the Devil's."

My face was twisted up. "I'm in the blood of Christ," I repeated. "You're a false prophet."

"What did you say?" George moved in front of the window like a black hole swallowing the view of the cows.

"You're a false prophet. You're a wolf in sheep's clothing," I repeated.

George clenched his fists. In a second they were open and fluttering like the ghosts of dead birds above his head. "You're lost," he said.

"Right," I said. "I'm lost. Right," I repeated.

"This meeting is over."

"Fine," I said. The woman suddenly appeared. Was she taller?

"Come with me," George said. He brought me out in front of the deacons gathered on the front porch. The deacons were still there talking about football. They stared at me. "This man has renounced

Christ." George gestured at me. "He is apostate." No one stirred. No one spoke up. The preacher with whom I'd eaten lunch every day for six months nodded his head gravely. I looked at them. Turned and walked out. In my truck I waited for something to happen. No one came out. I drove off. I still have the planchette on my desk, sitting on top of my grandfather's books like a diva come out of the box.

PURE

Produced and Packed by

A. C. Shelton
Jacksonville, Ala.

Net Wt. _____

The Stars beneath Alabama

What Proust began so playfully became awesomely serious. He who has once begun to open the fan of memory never comes to the end of its segments. No image satisfies him, for he has seen that it can be unfolded, and only in its folds does the truth reside—that image, that taste, that touch for whose sake all this has been unfurled and dissected; and now remembrance progresses from small to smallest details, from the smallest to the infinitesimal, while that which it encounters in these microcosms grows even ever mightier. Such is the deadly game that Proust began so dilettantishly, in which he will hardly find more successors than he needed companions.

—Walter Benjamin, "A Berlin Chronicle"

The town square was a quarter mile from my grandparents' house on Pelham Road. All the big trucks headed north on Alabama Highway 21 came through this square. There was a cluster of small businesses bunched around this grass island: a hardware store with a toy display in the front window; two barber shops; two drugstores with lunch counters, one had a Ouija board for sale over the counter with a specter reaching out from the dark; two dime stores facing each other across the square like two male hyenas on Noah's Ark; a beauty shop; a department store condensed into a one-story rectangle with merchandise stacked vertically eight feet high; a dress shop; a gas station; and a bank owned by the local ruling-class family. The architecture was Federal style. Most of the buildings were built during Reconstruction. They were squat, boxlike structures that looked like pieces of a child's dollhouse arranged around a large dinner plate. An IGA grocery store was part of the square's frame coming into town from the south. On the other side were an auto supply store, a used car lot, and Zuma's Café. The town hall was visible on a side street running off to the east, and on two parallel lines in sight of each other were the Episcopal and the Presbyterian churches shooting up into the sky like two rockets headed for Jesus. A mule leg from the courthouse was the library where my grandmother worked.

The square was the mechanical heart of the town. The stitch by stitch commercial money was generated here before the businesses thinned into an icehouse, a shoe repair shop, and a dry cleaner. The Dairy Queen was just down the hill off the square. A few gas stations lingered on the main highways. A neighborhood grocery store near the train tracks was packed in between houses. The Rocket Drive-in sat two miles out of town on a flat straightaway. I ate three foot-long hot dogs with chili in the back of my grandmother's blue Buick there when I was six years old. She told me I had a hole in my stomach.[1] Grandmother ate everything, but in small portions. She drove fast though. I would fly my hand out of the car window, matching the speed of her blue Buick teardrop back to the house.

At the radial center of this heart like a stake driven into it was a marble statue of a Confederate infantryman looking north down Pelham Road. His rifle butt was propped on the ground for support. Around his chest was a bedroll. The soldier is just over six feet tall, perched on top of a ten-foot marble base. On the pedestal, the soldier looms over the World War I machine guns surrounding the base with their barrels pointing up in reverence. When I was six years old, my family moved from Southern California back to Jacksonville. I remembered the statue, but like it was the colossus in the ancient city of Rhodes whose open legs formed the entrance to the harbor. It had seemed gigantic. When we drove into town, it was December, but still warm. I saw a man that could have been a roly-poly bug tottering down the main street with a cane. My mother told me that this was my great-grandfather. Then through the car window I saw the statue, which had shrunk to fit the pages of the encyclopedia and the TV screen where I had seen the colossus. Now I have the opposite problem. The statue is just as unstable, but in feet and inches and smaller details. The bedroll may or may not be there. I have a plastic Confederate soldier, the only survivor from a set of forty Civil War soldiers, that has a bedroll strung around his body. He stands in a menagerie of dinosaurs, German knights, trains, and zeppelins in a toy cabinet hanging in my son's room. He has joined up with the statue like two stragglers heading home after Appomattox. My grandmother used to say things come in threes. I just can't see myself in the picture. I must be the third man coming home, a figure somewhere between a toy plastic soldier and marble.

I have been away from home for thirteen years, but it seems far longer, like the time between a child's Christmases that has been stretched into a hundred years. My mother died in 1996, followed in the fall of that year by my grandmother Shelton. I sold my farm in the last phase of my divorce settlement. My dog died. For a seven-year stretch I lived in Des Moines; the Finger Lake District in western New York; in Walla Walla, Washington; against the Blue Mountains in the Southeast; Tacoma, Washington, on the coast; Las Vegas; and Buffalo. I have trouble distinguishing things I dreamed and things I did; a consequence of my internal clock being scrambled by how each different apartment in each city always looked identical once my things were arranged into the specific constellation I lived under. The same books were piled in stacks against the wall in three-to-four-foot towers. I have no shelves. The wooden desk made from lumber salvaged from a barn stands on four slender legs cut from a four-by-four against the window with a ladder-back chair with a seat woven out of baling twine scooted under the desk. The chair is over a hundred years old, handmade, and uncomfortable, but my mother gave it to me. Then there was a pair of straight-back rocking chairs, graceful and approaching delicate if the body goes over 150 pounds. A four-by-two-foot rug from Persia before the fall of the Shah lies like a picture on the floor, complemented by a collection of collage pieces on the wall and a postcard rack on a swivel. All I had could be stashed in the bed of my Toyota one-ton truck inside the camper shell. Each piece was chosen not for comfort or speed—I would have preferred Ikea—but because each piece would condense into a fog rolling through my apartment as if it were across the pasture behind my farmhouse, swallowing the bottoms of the alders and willows along the creek and squeezing the longleaf pines into deep green banks in the sky. For me the zodiac wheel was perpetually turned to the sign of Saturn against an imaginary Alabama landscape. The problem is more complicated than my being away from home. Even at home I was away.

In the first part of the twentieth century an obscure German scholar who was denied his terminal degree, which would have granted him entrance into the university system, who made his living writing small pieces for journals and scripts for a radio show for children, wrote an autobiographical essay about his childhood in Berlin in the years before World War I. This was Walter Benjamin. He spent his life going home to a place that no longer wanted him or even existed. In many ways this is an odd reading of Walter Benjamin's career. He is more often identified with the Paris of his later work and not the nostalgia for his childhood home. But Benjamin's nostalgia for home was not conventional. He yearned for a magic inside his own childhood in toys, books, and in a constellation of objects. His nostalgia was different from Proust's. Benjamin had strong Kafka-like currents and a polite brutality that informed his work. In Proust this was manifested in the tourniquet of gossip; in Benjamin's work it was a state of emergency activated by the Gestapo. He grew up in a middle-class Jewish family in a fashionable district. His father owned a department store that became a dominant motif in Benjamin's writing as a spatial intersection of dreams and commodities and culminated in his masterwork, the unfinished *Arcades Project*. At its simplest, the work is a history of nineteenth-century Paris centered on the glass and iron shopping districts, known as the arcades, the forerunners to the department store.[2] At the other extreme, it is a kabbalah-like history based on fluid samples of capitalism itself, whose object was messianic—to awaken the dreamer in the twentieth century. Benjamin said he wrote under the sign of Saturn, though closer up the constellation would have resembled a department store display filled with collections of objects arranged into weird juxtapositions.

When he completed the provisional draft of "A Berlin Chronicle," a nostalgic look homeward in 1932, Benjamin was already forty years old and a refugee. Berlin was receding from him like the sand

under his feet at the edge of the surf. The account is a Proustian remembrance of his childhood home that is not punctuated by vivid
recollections but stalked by figures[3] slowly emerging from a myopic
fog. The effect the text creates is like gradually becoming aware of
a bright green praying mantis in the setting of flowers on the table.[4]
Nothing particular happened to the young Benjamin, but extraordi-
nary or melodramatic events were not the object of "A Berlin Chronicle." The essay focuses on the dense landscape of memory, with its
lush vegetation and fauna, and its encroachment into the present.[5]
In his essay on Proust, Benjamin momentarily adopts an insect metaphor to describe the tenacity and voraciousness of Proust's extrac-
tion of memory. "Proust's most accurate, most conclusive insights
fasten on their objects the way insects fasten on leaves, blossoms,
branches, betraying nothing of their existence until a leap, a beating
of wings, a vault, show the startled observer that some incalculable
individual life has imperceptibly crept into an alien world."[6] The
metaphor emphasizes qualities and dangers often overlooked in the
reconstruction of memories. Proust's project is not a dainty exer-
cise, but a strenuous, powerful desire within an ecological system.
But the beetle in the account is herbivorous and not carnivorous. It
is the sticky feet of the leaf-eating beetle that grip and not the jaws or
the forearms of the mantis stalking the beetle.[7] Benjamin himself was
more of a solitary wood beetle[8] in looks and temperament.[9] There
is a famous photograph of Benjamin hunched over a table in the
Paris library extracting the samples that made up *The Arcades Project*. He is slope-shouldered, chubby, sprouting a heavy mustache as
if it were a sex organ. He is wearing a dark, musty suit—it must have
been soaked in tobacco smoke. The camera catches him munch-
ing unawares. Underneath his exoskeleton his muscles were softly

saddled in lard, only his thumb and forefinger like toy pincers had bite. What graphic violence there is in Benjamin's work occurs outside the text in his life or just past the sentence in what is implied. It is Benjamin the beetle who is the object of the violence, unaware of or resigned to what is materializing around him. His soft beetle eyes, the spongy wood, the methodical chewing into the past as future, all make him vulnerable to what is around him. He was on a Gestapo list. Benjamin's recollections are in a soft focus throughout most of "A Berlin Chronicle," but there is something acidic in the hazy retelling.[10] The writing quickly spreads to something more supernatural. Heart-shaped structures start to dissolve in a ghost world of memories, dreams, and fading cameos of relationships, ending with this scene that is filled with a cool fog and something sharp:

> I was perhaps five years old. One evening—I was already in bed—my father appeared, probably to say goodnight. It was half against his will, I thought, that he told me the news of a relative's death. The deceased was a cousin, a grown man who scarcely concerned me. But my father gave me the news with details, took the opportunity to explain, in answer to my question, what a heart attack was, and was communicative. I did not take in much of the explanation. But that evening I must have memorized my room and my bed, the way you observe with great precision a place where you feel dimly that you'll later have to search for something you've forgotten there. Many years afterwards, I discovered what it was. Here in this room, my father had "forgotten" part of the news about the deceased: the illness was called syphilis.[11]

By the end of Benjamin's essay, the camouflaged praying mantis has slipped from the flowers to the sleeve and has crawled up the arm and is poised motionless on the shirt collar by the throat.[12] The vivid recollection of memory is indefinitely postponed. But Benjamin achieves something else in the essay. There is a haunted, luxuriant quality to the narrative that is torn to pieces before the reader's eyes. The essay is just one of the small pieces Benjamin wrote that were groping toward his enormous mapping of the dead Paris in *The Arcades Project;*[13] dead in that every figure, including himself, is alternately fading away or turning into allegory. "A Berlin Chronicle" is a ghostly parlor set down in the desert of a children's book. There are still actors even if they are trapped in Benjamin's childhood. Sand is mixing with the Persian rugs. An adder is sliding around the loveseat's curved legs. The gas lamps are extinguished by Bedouin tribesmen who look through the family seated in the upholstered chairs as if they were but a small dust cloud. Mr. Benjamin makes a similar point, straight out within the essay:

> I wish to write of this afternoon, because it made so apparent, what kind of regimen cities keep over imagination, and why the city—where people make the most ruthless demands on one another, where appointments and telephone calls, sessions and visits, flirtation and the struggle for existence grant individuals not a single moment of contemplation—indemnifies itself in memory, and why the veil that has been covertly woven out of our lives *shows the images of people, far less than those of the sites of our encounters with others or ourselves.* Now on the afternoon in question I was sitting inside the Café des Deux Magots at St. Germain-des-Près, *where I was waiting—I forget for whom.*[14]

First the faces and then the bodily assemblages like the shoulder and jacket recede and vanish until there is the empty parlor, which slowly turns to rolling dunes of sand. Benjamin was an avid collector of children's books and toys. These collections may have functioned for him as a wall to hold his memories intact. Like Kafka's *"The Great Wall of China was finished off at its northernmost corner. From the southeast and the southwest it came up in two sections that finally converged there. This principle of piecemeal construction was also applied on a smaller scale by both of the two great armies of labor, the eastern and western. It was done in this way: gangs of some twenty workers were formed who had to accomplish a link, say, five hundred yards of a wall, while a similar gang built another stretch of the same length to meet the first. But after the juncture had been made the construction of the wall was not carried on from the point, let us say, where this thousand yards ended; instead, the two groups of workers were transferred to begin building again in quite different neighborhoods. Naturally in this way many great gaps were left, which were only filled in gradually and bit by bit, some, indeed, not till after the official announcement that the wall was finished. In fact, it is said there are gaps which have never been filled in at all, an assertion, however, that is probably merely one of the many legends to which the building of the wall gave rise, and which cannot be verified, at least by any single man with his own eyes and judgment, on account of the extent of the structure."*[15] Benjamin's memory wall is built in sections unconnected to other pieces like a mouth being constructed a tooth at a time with gaps on either side of the solitary tooth. He wouldn't be the first to use collections for memory storage and preservation. Marcel Proust's apartment was crammed with his family's furniture. I doubt whether Berlin could be found intact in Walter's collection or Proust's beloved childhood home in the piles of furniture stacked like cordwood in the spare rooms. *"Unable to relinquish completely the object of his deepest affections, Proust left the family apartment, but refused to part with his parents' furniture. Resisting his brother Robert's suggestion that the family heirlooms be put up for sale, Proust transported as much furniture to Boulevard Haussmann as the smaller apartment could hold, putting another three roomfuls in storage. The goal for Proust in retaining these painful reminders of life . . . was to reconstitute the very place he initially sought to escape, 'the place where Mama rests.'*"[16] My past persists in the broken foundations in the middle of a pecan orchard slumped with dirt and overgrown with privet and daylilies, a pile of bricks where the chimney was, a broad slate hunk that was the stoop to the side door, a colony of rusty nails burrowed into the first six inches of dirt, deformed into a botanical and mineral skeleton of a house that was here.

On my grandfather's farm there were several house sites from different eras scattered across the pastures and hickory woods. What had been a smattering of farms were by the 1930s consolidated into larger estates. Some of the pastures still carried their dead owners' names even though their home sites were piles of bricks and orange eruptions of daylilies. My grandfather died in 1986. His last home is still standing. A chicken farmer lives there.

The ruins are different. They decay from the inside out as the memories become unwrapped from the still existing shapes. While from the outside the house looks virtually identical to the one my grandfather lived in, on the inside there is an accelerating decay that is not about the literal walls or the ceiling joists. There are no termites; my own memories are rotting, leaving only a hard physical shell in the landscape. Toward the end of his life Granddad started selling real estate again. He specialized in farmland. I would occasionally have to drive him out to meet potential buyers. He treated the car like it was a shed. Baling twine was curled in long knots on the floorboards. A steel bucket sat in the backseat. Feed sacks lay on old newspapers. Cow medicine in plastic bottles, a tattoo kit in a plastic tackle box, and feed corn scattered on the seat were all mixed together in a Pentecost. On these trips he would be dressed in a suit and tall, black rubber boots. Turning to me from the passenger seat of the car, he told me, "Allen, you know all this land is being bought up by Arabs." In his living room were my grandmother's copies of the *Arabian Nights* discreetly shelved right next to *The Prophet*. Only now do I see the Bedouins extinguishing the lights in the parlor.

My grandfather A. C. Shelton was a tall man just over six feet two. He seemed larger because of how small the objects he kept near his person were. He carried a child-sized pocketknife. He wore a thin leather belt and favored delicate half boot, half shoes. He was inseparable from a slender, candy cane–shaped cattle stick, and instead of a truck drove a short, boxy Buick sedan around the farm. At his heaviest he approached 180 pounds, though his waist was almost as thick as his chest. He stood perpendicular to the ground, a peculiar reminder that he was for a time a mathematics professor and that he was the decisive line in the algorithm of pieces wherever he was. In photographs, his head is perched like a long-necked ibis staring into space over the others. From the side, the slightest slope of his shoulder was noticeable, which looked like the first turn of the pharaoh crossing his arms in death. It was hard to tell whether he was going into or coming out of a deep sleep even as a young man. He wore his hair the same way he did when he was twenty-five. The flanks of his head were shorn to the skin and cut straight across as if he were part of a monastic order. His resemblance to a holy man was accentuated by the buttoned top on his shirt collar and the way he carried his cattle stick crooked around his arms folded at his waist. AC looked like he was expecting to walk through the Resurrection like it was a tall grass pasture filled with thistle, swinging at the weeds with his stick.

In his bedroom, his height and posture were out of place. It was too small. He was stuffed into the room like a lanky hound in a plywood doghouse in the backyard. The room was ten feet by twelve feet. Laid on the floor with his arms over his head in a backstroke, there was a two-foot margin on the east-west axis and four feet along the north-south. Standing outstretched to the ceiling, there was another two feet. Only still, as a pillar of salt in the wilderness, did the ratio of space expand. There was an iron bed covered in a thin mattress stuck in the room's gut. The pores of the faded Persian rug were saturated with his odor and were laid on top of another layer of carpet that covered the concrete pad, which was the floor. Even after he died the room smelled like he had just come in from the cows. The bed was the same one he had slept in for forty years. The mattress was imprinted with the indentation of his shoulders and hips. The bedspread filled the cavity in the mattress. The imprint of his body looked like an angel shorn of his wings curled up in a fetal position. At his death the room was closed off from the air conditioning and the hallway. Because of this the room went on just as if he were alive, breathing and smelling of him. Marcel Duchamp called this the "infra-thin," where a body touches an object and forms an infinitesimal membrane that is a hybrid of both. Duchamp gave as examples from the early twentieth century corduroy pants mixed with thighs or tobacco smoke and lips smelling of each other. Here the presence Duchamp imagined was not singular, but a colony filling the room, an infra-thin the size of a giant prehistoric sloth's carcass stretched into a quivering membrane over the Persian rug and pinned to the floor with the bed's four iron legs. AC was being composed in that room. He was methodically given up to the swirls of dust in the narrow bands of light. And with him the map of my grandfather that was drawn was slowly disintegrating. The map[17] of the arrangement of the room was so detailed that it ended up covering the territory of my grandfather exactly (the decline of AC witnesses the fraying of his double, little by little, stretching and falling into ruins, though some shreds are still discernible in the room—the metaphysical beauty of this ruined abstraction, testifying to a pride equal to a young AC standing in front of his college math class, the map rotting like a carcass, returning to the substance of the floor; the double ends by being confused with the real through aging) as the most beautiful allegory of simulation. This fable has now come full circle and possesses nothing but the discreet charm of second-order simulacra, a cattle stick propped against the corner by the door of an empty house. AC's room kept him a molding ghost in a refrigerated empire at the back of the house. Occasionally pieces were ripped out for redistribution to my relations. Other objects waited for the landfill dolefully, emptied of all value except space.

The closet in this room was the same size as the wardrobe that would have stood in the corner of the house in which he had grown up. A foot and a half deep and four feet wide inside, it mimicked an upright coffin. He grew up in a ramshackle dogtrot house with rough pine siding. There would have been no closets in this space. Each room was ruthlessly rectangular.[18] After his death, stray objects were put away in drawers or piled inside the closet. In the closet his suits hung like hides that had been drying for years. His pants were long cotton tears slipping off the wire hangers. His shirts ached for oxygen. The king of that cramped space was AC's tuxedo. The other clothes were pushed back six inches on their hangers so that nothing touched its blackness. The tuxedo was a formal, double-breasted outfit. He had bought it for official occasions at the state legislature in Montgomery. He was a state senator for fourteen years. My grandmother insisted I take it. We were close in size, she assured me, even though I was three inches shorter and broader. On me there was a long drop in the crotch. AC wore his pants high on his waist. The tuxedo lay on me like a sleeping black animal whose muscles had gone slack.

In the pocket of the tuxedo jacket were two cuff links with the seal of Alabama emblazoned on the face, and a small envelope. The pocket had a fleshy feeling. While I can't recall what my grandfather's hands felt like, I can still recall how the smooth lining of the jacket felt. Inside the envelope was a photocopy of a newspaper article neatly folded to fit exactly the envelope's shape like a well-designed relationship. Across the top printed in all capital letters was the name of the paper, "The Livingston Gazette," and the date, October 11, 1919. The writing was not AC's. The writing was delicate and had cursive flourishes. It was a woman's handwriting, but whose? Was the writing his secretary's at the insurance company? Could it have been his sister, who still lived in the area? There was no writing of any kind on the envelope that would provide a second coordinate to fix the identity of the author. It could have been from my grandmother. My grandparents were never publicly affectionate. The rare occasion for the heart where their hands or shoulders actually touched took place in the architectural emotion crafted for a formal photograph. The envelope was a plain, white business envelope like the kind strewn across office desks. The letter was a reminder that there were things I couldn't quite imagine in my grandfather's life that were rolling up to the surface like a sea monster. AC didn't carry photographs in his wallet. There were no photographs on his desk at work or at home. The closest thing there was to a sentimental attachment was over my grandfather's desk at home. It was a three-by-four-foot reproduction of a relief, facing out from Stone Mountain near Atlanta, that showed the mighty trinity of the defeated Confederacy. The generals Robert E. Lee and the martyred Stonewall Jackson with his beaver-tail-sized beard flank the defeated President Jefferson Davis. All three are mounted on horseback. This sentimental portrait of the glorious South had no connection to AC except as a business sign signifying a form of commercial stability. He had no reverence for this lost world.[19]

AC grew up in the out-of-the-way town of Livingston on the edge of the Mississippi state line at the northern terminus of the Black Belt and just west of the University of Alabama in Tuscaloosa. When he was young there were still open ranges and big stretches of swampland. He rounded up stray cows in the swamps for money and delivered mail on horseback. There was a teaching college there where AC got his bachelor's degree before heading to Nashville and Peabody College. Livingston was an abstract space without any specificity. It was as far away as my grandfather's belly button. I never saw AC without his shirt. No matter how hot it was, his sleeves were at his wrist and the top button at his throat was fastened. Even in August while running cows, he wore a long-sleeved shirt and undershirt, like an iron skin prosthetic in the broiling Alabama sun. His skin was as white and creamy as a grub. I never heard him say anything about how he missed his home or wanted to go back for a visit. That part of the world seemed to be dead except for this clipping. He spent his life without ever seeing the ocean or the Mississippi River.

I read the copy of the article three times at increasingly slower speeds until I was mouthing each word, trying to find a name I recognized or a thread that tied him to the paper. There was no angle I could see that intersected the world I knew of AC. The article was an account of the faculty wives' club at Mrs. Arnold's home on the afternoon of October 11. It was the guest speaker's birthday. AC was born on Columbus Day. Was that the clue I was looking for? The speaker was a missionary from China. She was touring the United States raising money for her mission in a province outside Beijing. Her name was Esther Humphries. She'd grown up in Tonawanda, a community bordering Buffalo, New York. Max Weber, the German sociologist, had visited the area during his tour of the United States in 1905 and interviewed German workers along the docks and lumberjacks in Tonawanda. It seems he too had a China fantasy that permeated his work. What began with these interviews and culminated in *The Protestant Ethic and the Spirit of Capitalism* had a magnetic needle that pointed to China. China stands behind the United States in Weber's work like Kublai Khan's daughter behind a silk screen. Who was behind this clipping? Esther had survived what was described by the American papers as the Chinese *Titanic*. Three hundred people drowned in the China Sea when their ship capsized in a storm. She described how the lights from the ship looked like stars in the water as it rolled beneath the waves. She had thought of Peter, and when he had walked on the water during the storm, how Jesus grabbed his hand as he sank. Esther led the survivors in devotional hymns until they were rescued by a British steamer. She sang one of them for the gathering without accompaniment. The column quoted her reciting the scriptural verse about doing God's work and leaving one's home and family. She recounted her epiphany at the Pan-American exhibition where her imagination and zeal for the Lord were fired by the exhibitions from China. She described the cultivation of a prayer garden at her mission. The Chinese garden reproduced the flowers and shapes that surrounded her childhood home. Buffalo and her family were always in her heart. There was an announcement of next week's meeting, who provided the refreshments, and a thankful reportage on Mrs. Arnold's generous hospitality—and with that, the article stopped abruptly like a door closing.

When I showed the clipping to my grandmother she shrugged and passed it off as an interesting curio. "Your grandfather must've taken classes with Professor Arnold." A week later, she had a stroke. Her tongue was tied in a spit-soaked ribbon. No one could tell me what the intersection was. I was left with the lure of arriving at the beginnings of a memory that I never had. I was looking at a vanishing point like a swimmer at the edge of the horizon sliding under the water. My grandfather had articulated a dream or a fantasy about a life utterly foreign to him, not in his own handwriting, but in a copy of a newspaper clipping stuffed inside an envelope inside another pocket in a haunted closet. It was a complicated network of exchanges that my grandfather purloined in his tiny bedroom. But in the tragedies that followed a woman to China and back to Alabama, AC must have found something he could cling to as if it were he about to drown. She was a scrap of paper designed just for him. This tuxedo was a man in an oblong box floating in an ocean.[20]

The clipping drew me into a psychic seascape. It was a letter from the dead. Freud opens his book *Civilization and Its Discontents* with a story about a series of letters exchanged between himself and a friend. The literal contents of the letters are never given. I had a clipping in an unaddressed envelope with no idea about the transmission link. Freud traces out the shape of a disagreement between himself and his correspondent on the source of religious feelings. My grandfather and I argued about black pepper. Freud is crab-walking toward the gradual transformation of the letter into a psychic landscape and then finally into the city of Rome. Freud posits the city as a metaphor for the mind. Rome inexorably draws the earlier themes, images, and the letters Freud discussed into its gates. Like a molten marble vortex, Rome pulls everything back into its empire, including Freud. Seen from the center of the empire, the letters are paper simulations of the ancient city itself slowly turning back into marble. Freud sees in Rome a multidimensional hologram of the mind in which all the pasts continue to persist and jut into the present like unruly obelisks. The clipping I had in my hand was just as multidimensional and with no less a simulation of a capital of a world empire. But in this simulation the capital was more powerful and older than Rome—Beijing towers in the clipping. It was into this whirlpool my grandfather and I, a little ac, were sucked.

I have no idea who Esther Humphries was other than the brief description of her life given in the clipping. And now the clipping itself is gone, lost probably in a pile of papers stuffed in a garbage sack during my divorce. It is just as likely that my grandfather didn't know who Esther was other than through the same newspaper clipping. Her visit to Livingston was very brief. He could have seen her at the train station from a distance or at Professor Arnold's house. Professor Arnold was, as my grandmother pointed out, one of his teachers. So there is the possibility that he actually met her in passing. But AC was inexperienced in such social circumstances. He told me, "You can just as easily love a rich girl as a poor one. Always carry mouthwash with you and use it after a kiss." The mystery is not who she was or why the clipping was kept in his pocket. Other than his desk drawer in which he regularly kept his business records, the closet was the only private space he had. By the time he died it had been twenty years since he had worn the tuxedo. The tuxedo lay in his closet like an embalmed animal clutching this clipping as its heart.[21] And if that were so, the clipping may have hibernated in his pocket alone for years without ever being touched until I opened it. The mystery is sunk back into the acidic fog that is eating my memories from the inside until only shapes of AC remain. Esther is a kind of pressure almost materializing into a face in the mist.

I have the pine table that AC sat at for meals. It is a six-foot-by-two-foot pine rectangle that moved only three times in fifty years—from his house in town to the farm, then into my house, before being held even more still in a storage shed. AC never moved. He always sat facing west at a window to a pasture. He didn't engage in small talk. The closest was when he and I would argue about how I peppered my food. He was horrified by how I blackened my poached eggs. It will kill you, he'd tell me. In response I would point out that if not for the pepper we wouldn't be here. Christopher Columbus was looking for Chinese pepper. I'm only doing my part to commemorate history. AC was born on Columbus Day, but without his inclination to travel. He never knew I had fantasies about becoming a Marco Polo. Esther Humphries was produced for me. Her production was no different from the commodities Marx describes in *Capital* or the hoecakes Grandmother made. Esther was produced on a typewriter with x number of vowels and consonants ending in a set number of words, at a specific wage per hour. Behind this page screen, her production is more complicated, but still governed by the iron law of hours and dollars. Her value was not in her shape or form. I could only imagine this. She was like the coat or the iron bar Marx writes about in his equation; one coat equals twenty pounds of linen, which equals x number of iron bars. She had no specificity except as a position in an exchange system. Her specificity shifts like the image of the parlor swallowed by the desert sand. Esther was not tangible. She was already a spectral image, even in the world contained inside the society column. Esther's value was inside the form, in the secret spaces where I was Marco Polo exploring an empire as far-reaching as the Empire of China. Here is where Esther flickers and shivers like a light on the horizon, or what Proust called his magic lantern that cast images on his childhood's bedroom wall, or what Benjamin described as a phantasmagoria.[22] Esther's one-dimensionality is deceptive. She is a sheet that can be passed through. Esther was a letter from someone summoning me to a castle.

> It was late in the evening when ac arrived. The farm was deep in snow. My grandfather's house on the hill was hidden, veiled in mist and darkness, nor was there even a glimmer of light to show that a house was there. On the wooden bridge leading from the main road to the farm, ac stood for a long time gazing into the illusory emptiness above him.

Kafka's character K. never arrives at the castle. By the end of the novel the writing itself is swallowed by the fog that obscures the castle, and what little text is there is beginning to disintegrate from contact with the acid. The novel doesn't just end in midsentence; it is being consumed back to the very beginning, erasing K. to a blank space. No wonder AC kept a strict regimen. It was an assertion of boundaries against a slow erasure.

What Esther touched off was the destabilization of space and distance. A letter becomes a castle. A door is an envelope. Memory pulls and sucks like a thick muck on a body. The swamp changes distance into depth and slime. Marx opens his massive excursive on the Kafka-like castle, Capital, with this disarmingly simple observation that belies the swamp-like quality of Capital: *"The wealth of societies in which the capitalist mode of production prevails appears as an 'immense collection of commodities'; the individual commodity appears as its elementary form. Our investigation therefore begins with the analysis of the commodity."*[23] What makes this opening turn alternately mysterious and perfectly lucid is Marx's authorial posture. In the first paragraph he stands like K., the surveyor before the edifice of Capital. Marx likens himself to a physicist and begins the process of dismantling the castle into its elementary or molecular units—a multitude of commodities. He doesn't begin with a description of squalid working conditions or an account detailing the monstrous crushing of children in the factories;[24] he begins with what would be the clouds in Kafka's account—the banks of commodities that fill everyday life like a literal fog. Still, there is no mystery that threatens to turn into a storm churning the clouds of commodities into immense thunderheads. It is what Marx proposes next that leads him into an underworld that is filled with danger. Marx begins the first solo descent into the commodity and into the system that expands and moves like a sky or an ocean between them. The last sentence in volume 1 of *Capital* makes this clear: *"The only thing that interests us is the secret discovered in the New World by the political economy of the Old World, and loudly proclaimed by it: that the capitalist mode of production and accumulation, and therefore capitalist private property as well, have for their fundamental condition the annihilation of that private property, which rests on the labor of the individual himself; in other words, the expropriation of the worker.*"[25] The Atlantic is bursting inside Marx's sentence, leaving the human like a conch pulled from its shell in the shallows.

For Marx the commodity, the elemental unit of capitalism, is a storage unit for humanness. This is the insight he used to solve the mystery of value. But it is not like a closet or a refrigerator. These spaces are too static. The commodity is closer to a vampirish freezer or the house Edgar Allan Poe imagines in "Tell-Tale Heart" that ticks like a heart swaddled in cotton or a watch stabbed deeply into an abdomen. *"It was a low, dull, quick sound—much such a sound as a watch makes when enveloped in cotton. I gasped for breath—and yet the officers heard it not"* (my emphasis). The dead old man and the murderer were incorporated into the house. In keeping with Marx's documentation of the commodity, the murdered remain largely anonymous. There are no names in this Poe account, and only rarely does a named individual bob to the surface in Marx. The phrase "the introjection of labor" is too antiseptic to describe the engorging of the human into the commodity. The commodity soaks up humanness. Personal memories dissolve on contact with the subterranean ocean inside the commodity. Memories are mixed together in a Babel that soars inward. Marx repeats these images in his famous description of the anonymously possessed table stalking about in his description of commodity fetishization. *"The form of wood, for instance, is altered if the table is made out of it. Nevertheless, the table continues to be wood, an ordinary, sensuous thing. But as soon as it emerges as a commodity, it changes into a thing which transcends sensuousness. It not only stands with its feet on the ground, but in rela-*

tion to all other commodities, it stands on its head, and evolves out of its wooden brain grotesque ideas, far more wonderful than if it were to begin dancing of its own free will."[26] Neither the table nor spirits animating the table have names or an identity. The workers who made this table are strangers in a strange land, inhabiting parlors or dressing rooms of houses unimaginable from inside a wooden coffin.

In Marx's reading of the living conditions of workers in London in the 1860s, he concentrates on the physical dimensions that encase the workers. The measurements are meticulously given us, as are the cubic feet of oxygen available. But Marx shies away from the person like a pupa burrowed into these tight spaces. Marx calculates their life spans running from point to point, mirroring his estimation of the generation of surplus value. Here it would seem to be an anti-surplus, a life running in the negative. The human dimension is not part of the text except in strategic strokes like his description of the death of a seamstress:

In the last week of June 1863, all the London daily papers published a paragraph with a "sensational" heading, "Death, from simple over-work." It dealt with the death of the milliner, Mary Anne Walkey, 20 years old, employed in a highly respectable dressmaking establishment, exploited by a lady with the pleasant name of Elsie. The old, often-told story was now revealed once again. These girls work, on average, 16 1/2 hours without a break, during the season often 30 hours, and the flow of their fleeting "labor power" is maintained by occasional supplies of sherry, port or coffee. It was the height of the season. It was necessary, in the twinkling of an eye, to conjure up magnificent dresses for the noble ladies invited to the ball in honor of the newly imported Princess of Wales. Mary Anne Walkey had worked uninterruptedly for 26 1/2 hours, with sixty other girls, thirty in each room. The rooms provided only 1/3 of the necessary quantity of air, measured in cubic feet. At night, the girls slept in pairs in the stifling holes into which a bedroom was divided by wooden partitions. And this was one of the better millinery establishments in London. Mary Anne Walkey fell ill on the Friday and died on Sunday, without, to the astonishment of Madame Elsie, having finished off the bit of finery she was working on.[27]

Space is a wooden prosthetic suit that literally squeezes the air out of the workers and their families. Here is an example of Marx's measurements of the Poe-like rooms that surround the individual:

> Kennington, very seriously over-populated in 1859, when diphtheria appeared. . . . In one district, there stood four houses named birdcages; each had four rooms of the following dimensions in feet and inches:
>
> Kitchen: 9 ft 5 by 8 ft 11 x 6 ft 6
> Scullery: 8 ft 6 x 4 ft 6 x 6 ft 6
> Bedroom: 8 ft 5 by 5 ft 10 x 6 ft 3
> Bedroom: 8 ft 3 x 8 ft 4 x 6 ft 3[28]

What Marx achieves in the strange cubic descriptions is comparable to finding the architect's blueprint to the House of Usher. He finds in mathematical specifications a haunting and an emptiness that roll like the sound of the sea in an empty seashell. The rooms measure what is left of how the human vanishes in the cell-like cubicles within a carceral empire. The cramped spaces Marx finds are the turned-out interiors of commodities and record what happens to the human squeezed inside the commodity netherworld. In the 1973 French novel *Life: A User's Manual,* Georges Perec recalls the vanished and their residues in an abandoned apartment building. In one tiny side story, Perec writes:

> Its oval top, wonderfully inlaid mother-of-pearl, was exceptionally well pre-
> served; but its base, a massive, spindle shaped column of grained wood,
> turned out to be completely worm-eaten. The worms had done their work in
> covert, subterranean fashion, creating innumerable ducts and microscopic
> channels now filled with pulverized wood. No sign of this insidious labor
> showed on the surface. Grifalconi saw that the only way of preserving the
> original base—hollowed out as it was, it could no longer support the weight
> of the top—was to reinforce it from within; so once he had completely emp-
> tied the channels of their wood dust by suction, he set about injecting them
> with an almost liquid mixture of lead, alum, and asbestos fiber. The opera-
> tion was successful; but it quickly became apparent that, even thus strength-
> ened, the base was too weak, and Grifalconi had to resign himself to replac-
> ing it. . . . It was after he had done this that he thought of dissolving what was
> left of the original wood so as to disclose the fabulous arborescence within,
> this exact record of the worms' life inside the wooden mass: a static, min-
> eral accumulation of all the movements that had constituted their blind ex-
> istence, their undeviating single-mindedness, their obstinate itineraries; the
> faithful materialization of all they had eaten and digested as they forced from
> their dense surroundings the invisible elements needed for their survival, the
> explicit, visible, immeasurably disturbing image of the endless progressions
> that had reduced the hardest of woods to an impalpable network of crum-
> bling galleries.[29]

What are left are the hard parts. The body melts away like salty butter into emptiness. The plaster then captures the weird patterns in disappearances as something beautiful, as something that moves, from how worms track through wood to an allegory of how the human vanishes against architectural scaffolding. AC must have had an inkling of this when he was sitting next to a cluster of beehives and a bee crawled into his large ear and burrowed into the orange wax. If he reached up and smacked the bee, he would have been immediately stung by the hundreds of bees in the air. Bees release an odor when threatened by danger and AC was not quick. Once the bee was in the ear it chewed and pushed his earwax into a hexagon. More bees were drawn by the first buzzing and lighted on his ear. His whole head and then his torso could be transformed into a network of cells filled with honey. Beeswax would replace his brain and lungs inside a bone hive. The green clover pastures were turning into *"the agony of water. . . . The honey which slides off my spoon on to the honey contained in the jar first sculptures the surface by fastening itself on it in relief, and its fusion with the whole is presented as a gradual sinking, a collapse, which appears at once as a deflation and as display—like the flattening out of the full breasts of a woman who is lying on her back."*[30] In those moments, sitting Indian style in the pine woods with the bee inside his head, AC could have suspected that the bees were after that which was sticky inside him. After a few minutes of his sitting perfectly still the bee in his ear crawled back out. AC got up and walked out of the cluster of hives.

After a series of strokes, so small that they were only acknowledged in their cumulative effect, my grandfather was institutionalized in a nursing home that my uncle had built, that I had worked on as a laborer for $2.25 an hour, and on land that my grandfather had owned. AC was ill suited for this world. The only TV he watched was the news in the morning and evening, and on Saturday nights *The Lawrence Welk Show*. What he ate was regulated by a rigid code.

Every meal included honey, applesauce, rice, and a glass of tap water with no ice. Now I see the water as a simulation of what he imagined the ocean's temperature to have been off China. The room was roughly the same size as his bedroom, but his own smell was replaced by Lysol. The iron bed, the musty Persian rug were changed to gleaming steel and square tiles—surfaces without patina and incapable of absorbing him as a smell. The most severe change was in the ecological relationship of his room. Before, his room was like a doghouse for a hound, a place only for sleeping. Now it was a cell. At home, AC walked as much as ten miles a day checking the cattle herd. The pasture was his dream space. Without it, his thoughts must have collapsed on themselves. The distance between him and those around him was emphasized, leaving him like a passenger going down in the China Sea. He steadily starved himself to death. It took a month, but he had an iron will. The day of his death he was moved to the hospital and pumped with fluids to combat his dehydration. By 9:30 p.m. he was dead. By 10:15, I was staring at him in the soft light. The TV was blank. The white sheets that held his long skeleton seemed as rigid as steel.

The cotton formed a prison around AC, an iron maiden that clutched him to her breast. AC would not have been her first lover. Cotton's history has long been intertwined with what Michel Foucault described as the panoptic institutions as one of its basic molecular units. In much the same way as the pencil became a critical part of the deployment of discipline within the school, cotton's cost, washability, and the relative ease with which it can be bleached lent itself to the gathering together of these microhistories into that which makes up the necessary nursing home as something more than the simple stockpiling of old bodies. My grandmother called it the waiting room for the angel of death. In this context, the key word is waiting room, the foyer of the panoptic. But sleeping silently in the backrooms are the white sheets, drawn tautly over the gleaming beds. Unfurled on the floor, the sheets are like bodies without a skeletal system.

In Talcott Parsons's translation of *The Protestant Ethic and the Spirit of Capitalism,* Max Weber imagines a similar materiality hardening into a prison cell around the individual. Weber writes, "In Baxter's view the care for external goods should only lie on the shoulders of the 'saint like a light cloak, which can be thrown aside at any moment.' But fate decreed that the cloak should become an iron cage."[31] The cloak mentioned here would be linen or wool and not cotton, but this was not the important detail that Weber was after. Weber was tracing the development of a specific character that formed an enclosure as hard as steel around the self by the early part of the twentieth century. How this was materially manifested was not the kind of question that Weber tried to answer. The world capitalist economy in the sixteenth century was still unconsolidated. Large stretches of cultural enclaves, even within the future core states, were still not capitalized in terms of market or labor, one of Weber's key points. The light cloak lying on his saint is before the rise of cotton as the dominant materiality. It was the early nineteenth century before cotton was in widespread use across all classes as underwear, according to the French historian Fernand Braudel, which fed directly into the gathering hygienic movement that thrived on the discipline of the body, surfaces and the control of filth. India was the principal source of cotton cloth in the distinctive calico weave before the English took over the market. Nor could Weber fully grasp that the cotton sheet was part of the deployment of an institutional grip on the person that concretely held the person in an intersection of labor, commodity fetishization, and time schedules. And for all his fascination with China and America as strategic weights in the development of capitalism, he could not conceptualize the oceans that linked them to Europe. His was a dry analysis. In contrast is Marcel Proust's documentation of how "honey" grips a person in *Swann's Way*. The past reaches out in long vegetative tendrils to snare the individual. Proust's world is wet.

> . . . when one day in winter, as I came home, my mother, seeing that I was cold, suggested that, contrary to my habit, I have a little tea. I refused at first and then, I do not know why, changed my mind. She sent for one of those squat, plump cakes called petite madeleines that look as though they have been moulded in the grooved valve of a scallop-shell. And soon, mechanically, oppressed by the gloomy day and the prospect of a sad future, I carried to my lips a spoonful of the tea, in which I had let soften a piece of the madeleine. But at that very instant when a mouthful of tea mixed with cakecrumbs touched my palate, I quivered, attentive to the extraordinary thing that was happening in me. A delicious pleasure had invaded me, isolated me, without my having any notion as to its cause. It had immediately made the vicissitudes of life unimportant to me, its disasters innocuous, its brevity illusionary, acting in the same way that love acts, by filling me with a precious essence: or rather this essence was not in me, it was me. I had ceased to feel I was mediocre, contingent, mortal. Where could it have come to me from—this powerful joy? I sensed it was connected to the taste of the tea and the cake, but that it went infinitely far beyond it, could not be of the same nature. Where did it come from? What did it mean? How can I grasp it? I drink a second mouthful, in which I find nothing more than in the first, a third that

gives me a little less than the second. In time for me to stop, the virtue of the drink seems to be diminishing. It is clear that the truth I am seeking is not in the drink, but in me.[32]

Proust's famous tea and madeleine scene holds in its currents not only the narrator's past, but the unconscious of the capitalist empire. The sugar, the tea, the seashell-shaped cookie made by the servant, the plush setting in which the scene unfolds are made from how India and China were bound to France and the encroachment of the commodity world into everyday life. This scene is part of a wet empire of signs, which emphasizes how Weber landlocked his analysis of capitalism. Oceans, winds, ships, and "unconscious currents" are downplayed in his work. Consequently Weber missed that the iron cages encasing individuals are inevitably filled with literal fluids. The encasements act as collection points for runoffs of water, piss, and the green tea in Marcel's cup. Inside these iron cages the liquids roll into sucking whirlpools just as if they were great oceans even if they are the size of a hospital room or a teacup pulling poor Proust back in time. My grandfather drowned in a cell the size of a Cadillac's interior. In his hospital bed he was a stain on a white sheet to be cleaned up.

In the Kafka short story "The Metamorphosis," the central character Gregor Samsa, a traveling salesman who lives at home with his sister and parents, wakes up and finds himself a beetle. There are sock problems. He has six legs. There are communication and dietary problems. The only sounds he can make are a kind of gurgling. Strangely, he can't make even a chirping or whirring sound. But then Gregor becomes a beetle without any of the superhero attributes he could have acquired. Written in 1908 in Prague, the story would seem to be a concrete description of Weber's steel casing. Working back and forth like the hind legs of the beetle between the literal hard-shelled exoskeleton and the smooth hardness of Gregor's circumstances that trapped him, AC never had a single transformational night comparable to Gregor's. The small strokes were a slow cumulative process that nudged him into the nursing home, which makes his history read like a creeping Kafka story in which Gregor materializes as a beetle piece by piece. First his left butt cheek turns hard and shiny and then his chest turns into an architectural mock-up of a thorax before the last piece turns beetle. Kafka draws a transformative line that he doesn't push Gregor across. Gregor never loses his tortured humanness. But even without this literal metaphor of an exterior encasement, Kafka's characters are often both victims and cartographers of character determination and enclosure. How self-conscious AC was about his own enclosures is beyond my reach. I know that he adhered to a strict dietary and water temperature regime. But this is not as constrictive as what I imagined his projection outward into the pasture, his own green China Sea, was. The clipping was a window into a receding ocean, a fluid, and is manifested in the pastures and in the figure of the woman herself. In the opening to *One-Way Street,* Walter Benjamin dedicates the book: "This street is named Asja Lacis Street after her who as an engineer cut it through the author."[33] For my grandfather, there would be no street but an ocean. A hole would have unleashed a wave that would have carried him into a liquid pasture like the swamps where he rounded up cattle as a young man.

AC was seventy years plus when he built his dream house on the farm on the top of the small hill overlooking the two lakes. He had had bulldozers scrape for the trickle of a creek he diverted through the woods in a narrow ditch overgrown with cattail. It was a plain house; one story, brick exterior, aluminum canopy the size of an umbrella over the front door, engineered to be as economical as possible. There was nothing lavish about it. It looked exactly like the houses in the low-income project on the edge of town. There were three small bedrooms; once the beds were stuffed into the center of each there was no room left to move except with careful deliberation. One room each for my grandfather and grandmother and a guest room across from the dining room. The windows of his bedroom faced west and north into a rolling pasture and a bank of small oaks and sweet gums. But the shades were always drawn. Without a view the room was like a tiny cabin in the lower decks of a passenger liner. The kitchen was a long, narrow hallway held back from the dining room by the oven and a shoulder-high cabinet. Two and a half bathrooms, as Spartan and cheap as possible, were spread through the house. The bathroom nearest the side door smelled like the sickly sweet milk formula used for abandoned calves and moldy rubber boots. The ornamental living room was held in a deep glacier waiting to be partially thawed in some kind of apocalyptic event like the imaginary tea parties that my grandmother and an eccentric cousin would have on Sunday afternoons, dressed up in long gowns and hats like they were dolls. I was often the visitor to these teas. Suspended inside the glacier were a piano, a fireplace with a brass grate, my grandmother's collection of porcelain Madonnas, and an enormous photographic painting of a family posing outside a two-story house with a bicycle against a picket fence. They weren't anyone I knew. They had no names. They were just a fiction, something posed like a family. The painting dominated the wall over the piano. I kept imagining that they were somehow connected to my grandfather and that if I could only measure more accurately his prehistory, I would arrive at the solution and the whereabouts of the giant wheeled bicycle that stalked about in the painting.

AC owned a bluetick hound called Smoky. One of the few plea-
sures AC allowed himself was coon hunting. As a young man he
scoured the mountains at night hunting possums and raccoons. He
carried a big, boxy flashlight and a shotgun. He hadn't hunted in
years, but in his eighties he bought Smoky, a first-class coonhound.
He hunted maybe five times and never treed a coon. Smoky had a
nose for foxes and led AC in wide circles through the woods without
ever cornering one. After that Smoky and AC retired from nighttime
romps until Smoky got a taste for goat and started killing nannies at
night. Smoky was fed kitchen scraps under the carport in a brownie
pan. Hoecakes, pieces of fatty meat, field peas, and ruined milk were
mixed with dry dog food and dumped into the pan. What Smoky
didn't eat, the ants did. By morning the ants would be working in
swarms on the mounds of cornbread, cutting it into pieces to be carried back to the colony. Just before the next feeding, Grandma would
turn what was left of the food in the dish onto the compost heap and
then wash the ants stuck in the sticky glob off with a hose. The luke-
warm cornbread and the ruined milk mixture formed something like
Proust's cup of tea. But as a model for remembrance, the cornbread
emphasizes certain characteristics dormant in Proust's conceptualization. The cornbread hovers near the nonhuman. The food is decaying, steps away from the compost heap, a hound's mouth and an
ant intelligence fed on human scraps.

Occasionally, big hunks of cornbread were pushed to the side
of the pan, were spilled onto the ground, or ended up set on top
of the goo with its hard crust limiting the absorption of the grease
and milk. In the morning these pieces would look like mines with
the ants cutting the cornbread from the inside out. The cornbread
riddled with ants begins to resemble Kafka's moles in the underground castle ("*Then there would be noises in the walls, no insolent*

*burrowing up to the very Keep itself; then peace would be assured there
and I would be its guardian; then I would not have to listen with loath-
ing to the burrowing of the small fry, but with delight to something
that I cannot hear now at all: the murmurous silence of the Castle
Keep")*[34] pulled to the surface like the mole's dirt brain in an autopsy
with all its intricate passages visible. There is nothing comparable
to this in Proust's world where domesticated vegetation dominates
and there are no praying mantises or ants or even flies. AC patrolled
the pasture with a can of ant poison. He would jam his stick into the
mounds to open up a long hole and then shake the poison into the
hole. The colony might rise up a foot or more into a delicate cake-
like structure laced with tunnels, and then sink easily three feet into
the ground into a complicated maze work. Once all was opened, it
would fill with thousands of fire ants coming to the surface like a
shaken bottle of Coca-Cola. Proust's work never materializes into a
sinister castle; Marcel's bedroom is the center of a labyrinth that extends back into memories horizontally. Proust crafted a monumental
world laid on edge, spiraling into a void sideways.

The den contained a metal desk, a rolling metal chair, a junked
wooden desk in the corner with potted plants, my aunt's bland college art experiments stretched on canvases, a glass-fronted bookcase
with out-of-date law books, a two-foot-high, black bank safe in the
closet with three feet of newspapers on top, two slope-backed rocking chairs, and a sofa slumped against the wall. There were a TV
set and a fireplace. The surface of the desk had papers slid across it
in overlapping thin geological layers like sheets of mica pulled back
and relaid in a mosaic. There were a ceremonial pen that didn't work
stuck in a mount, a desk calendar, a cheap ballpoint pen from the
local bank, and rubber bands from the newspaper. There were no

personal items. No photographs. No recognizable mementos. The insides of the desk were no different—rubber bands, trays filled with pennies, and a palm-sized rubber eraser. There must have been other pieces in the scene, but my memory is pockmarked with blanks as if the eraser were a supernatural creature actively consuming the other pieces that could have been remembered. I have that eraser now in a box in a closet at my house. I have the picture of Stone Mountain that hung like a shadow of a ghost over the desk in a storage shed in Alabama. The chair was the kind a stenographer used in a big office complex. The chair had a green cushioned back arched on a metal frame with rollers on the splayed legs. The desk itself was battleship green with a Plexiglas covering over the surface. At the edges were stuck a calendar and an interest table to calculate payments.

AC sat here to keep the birth records of his registered Black Angus herd—who the sire was, the lineage of the cow, and the date of the calving. AC owned nearly 120 brood cows divided into the Warlick, the Barnwell, the Harper, and the Back Barn pastures. In each pasture there was a different bull. A strand of electric wire augmented the barbed wire separating the pastures. The pastures ranged in size from 70 to 120 acres. In the 1970s, a stylistic shift took place in the desired configuration of the Black Angus bull. The classic bull looked like Arnold Schwarzenegger on all fours. A giant, heavy chest plug supported by four short legs. The bull was a big, black block that could have been used to build an obsidian pyramid. The modern bull, influenced by the introduction of the Indian Brahma and the French Limousins, was long-bodied and tall. The shift caused major problems in calving. More episiotomies had to be performed. There were more breech births. The jumble of legs had to be straightened in the womb. The height of fences had to be extended. In a frenzy a cow or a bull could clear a four-strand barbed wire fence. Here at his desk AC presided over the genetic ocean of his cows, working on his records with a mathematics professor's diligence. His own ancestry was a foreign territory. AC was one-quarter Choctaw. He rarely spoke of his family. Instead, AC attempted to control genetics with discipline, his own Great Wall of China and standing army. On his seventy-fifth birthday, sitting at this desk, working with a pencil, AC wrote this letter to be sent to the local newspaper. He quietly formed another newspaper clipping rather than a personal letter to be saved by his grandchildren. I have this clipping framed and hanging in my kitchen:

The following is a letter written recently by independent gubernatorial candidate and former state senator A. C. Shelton, to his grandchildren on his 75th birthday.

This letter is being written to you on my 75th birthday with the hope that you may be as healthy as I am when you reach this age. I am as active physically and as mentally alert as I was twenty years ago. Only a few of my boyhood friends are living today while I am enjoying perfect health.

When I was the age of some of you I adopted resolutions and principles which have been followed diligently. I thought of my body as the temple of my soul and resolved that I would do nothing that would weaken or damage it. I even thought it would be irreligious and immoral to smoke or drink.

There are many more temptations today than I had to face and you will have to be stronger than I was to resist them. Many of your friends will not only be smoking and drinking but will be using dangerous drugs. I hope you will be strong enough to resist all temptations and especially that of using drugs. Too many young people are ruining their lives by experimenting with them.

One of my principles was that of being honest and fair. I have never made a promise that I could not fulfill. A newspaper man recently referred to me as being the most honest man in Alabama. I am proud to pass that heritage to you.

My chest swells with pride to be able to stand before other people and say that I had never smoked a cigarette nor taken a drink of whiskey. I also add to the statement that I do not even drink wine, beer, coffee, tea, or carbonated drinks. I eat properly, and not to excess.

I have tried to provide a living example for my children and grandchildren to follow. I hope you will pass this tradition onto readers. (A. C. Shelton, *Anniston Star,* October 20, 1970)

AC's desk was a machine. There was nothing extraneous. There were no ornaments. The rubber bands and the opened envelopes were like debris produced by a grinding wheel on a factory floor. The battleship color of the metal was perfectly consistent with the imaginary world AC worked with in full view. He and the desk thought in 8 percent bites, the morally acceptable amount of interest that should be charged. The rich colors that lurked behind this facade were carefully guarded. In Kafka's novel *America,* the young immigrant engineer Karl is drawn to his uncle's desk because of its machinelike quality and the imagined deep memories that are conjured up in its insides:

In his room there was an American writing desk of the very finest sort, one of the kind his father had been longing for for years, and had tried to find at an affordably cheap price in various auctions, without ever being able to afford one with his small means. Of course his desk was nothing like the so-called American desks that turn up at European auctions. For instance, the top part of it had a hundred different compartments of all sizes, so that even the President of the Union would have found room for each of his files in it, but even better in that it had an adjuster at the side, so that by turning the handle one could rearrange and adjust the compartments in whatever way one wanted or needed. Thin lateral partitions slowly descended to form the floors of newly created compartments or the ceilings of enlarged ones; with just one turn of the handle, the appearance of the top would be completely transformed, and one could do it either slowly or at incredible speed, depending on how one turned the handle. It was a very modern invention, but it reminded Karl vividly of the nativity scenes that were demonstrated to astonished children at the Christmas Fairs at home. Karl himself, warmly dressed, had often stood in front of these nativities, and had incessantly compared the turning of the handle, which an old man performed, with the effect it had on the scene, the halting progress of the three Kings, the shining star of Bethlehem, and the shy life in the holy stable. And always it had seemed to him as though his mother, standing behind him, wasn't following the events closely enough and he had pulled her to him, until he felt her against his back, and had drawn her attention to various more subtle manifestations by loud shouts, say a rabbit that was alternately sitting up and making to run in the long grass at the front, until his mother put her hand over his mouth and presumably reverted to her previous dullness. Of course, the desk hadn't been designed to recall such things, but the history of inventions was probably full of such vague connections as Karl's memory.[35]

The description points out that his uncle's desk is a machine for handling information. But then the passage switches and the desk becomes a machine for reaching back in time. Order and fog ooze from the desk's pores. The same desk calculates like a wooden computer and conjures up Christmas memories like scaring up a fat goose from the water's surface with its wings flapping and long neck stretched out. While I could see the computational grinding of AC's desk, Christmas was opaque. Esther could not be here. Even though as an object of memory she was perfectly consistent with Kafka's desk—a combination of rational practices, type fonts, and desire—Esther was a machine-produced unconscious. AC's desk's unconscious was the underneath of a one-dimensionality, a wooden Möbius strip. His desk was about business. Even his letter to his grandchildren is a civic, business statement rather than a personal letter. There it is, the desire for the oceanic, underneath, but part of the overt rationality the desk was dedicated to. The pastures and genetic pools, old swamps, persist in the tax records and the sire genealogies. Here was the China Sea.

To get there, AC sold to Mr. Brown what I as a child thought was a castle, an antebellum mansion with a wraparound porch and a second-floor balcony built in 1858. He bulldozed the house, the hill it rested on, the three giant magnolias, an oak the size of King Kong, and the meandering flower garden into dump trucks and hauled them off to the dump. He built a gas station. Once uncapped, the hill spewed emaciated ghosts. The last hundred years were erased in a speeded-up geological succession. Mr. Brown died of cancer and his service station went out of business to be replaced by a convenience store. But where was here? The home AC built was a memory palace designed to reproduce the house he'd grown up in. But it was not the house that would generate memories. It was how the house forced him out into the pastures rolling out from the front steps like an ocean that generated the memories. AC had no sentimentality about home. He had left them all to do something like God's work in the pastures and the swamps that drew him into a green simulation of the China Sea and the stars beneath Alabama.

Assembling Mary Pullen for a Cry

> He who seeks to approach his own buried past must conduct himself like a man digging. . . . For matter itself is only . . . a stratum, which yields only to the most meticulous examination what constitutes the real treasure hidden within the earth: the images, severed from all earlier associations that stand— like precious fragments or torsos in a collector's gallery—in the sober rooms of our later insights.
>
> —Walter Benjamin, "A Berlin Chronicle"

> I took . . . 3 tablespoons of mud from . . . a little pond; counting each plant as it grew; the plants were altogether 537 in number; and yet the viscid mud was all contained in a breakfast cup!
>
> —Charles Darwin, *Origin of Species*

It was ten in the morning when I started digging the grave. Earlier, at the funeral home, a man in a dark polyester suit with soft brown loafers instructed me on the required dimensions. He was very concerned whether I could do the work. A slipup would be embarrassing. A request like this was unexpected. They had a crew of men who normally did this work. He had very smooth skin. Didn't I need to be with my family during this time? His hair was starting to thin. I knew his daughter from the preschool where I told stories on rainy days. She was a little girl with glasses who liked frogs. Did he know how scary my stories were?

I laid out the eight-by-four-foot shape on the grass with a framing square and a carpenter's rule. I pushed a rail spike into the dirt at each corner. The ground made a fleshy sound. I lined the new grave up parallel to my grandfather's. Then I strung the template with twine. An angel peered out at me from a marble tombstone. I plucked the string. It buzzed. I sat down on the edge of the headstone and drew a bastard file across the spade's blade until it could cut a snake in half. I watched the lamb sleeping on a child's grave. Following the twine, I scribed a line in the grass with the spade. The word of God is a sword, I remembered. The grass over the grave was cut into carpet-like hunks and carefully laid at the top of the tarp where I would shovel the dirt. The tarp would keep the grass from being clotted with dirt during the cleanup after the burial. With the outward dimensions of the grave in place, I had what looked like an unopened door to a deep room. The grave is four feet deep by code, but it seems far deeper now in my memory as I think about looking out from the bottom at the sky while I was scraping the bottom flat.

The room opened with a pick and mattock followed by a long-handled shovel. Standing on the grave, a trench is dug at the end, and stepping back, sections are pushed out into the open space and then the process is repeated. The dirt was shoveled into a wheelbarrow, rolled to my pickup, shoveled onto the bed, and then dumped at the edge of the cemetery into bloodred piles. This is necessary because once the shovel unpacks the ground the dirt will no longer go back into the hole without reproducing the pressure that held the dirt and clay in place. The dirt expands in an overwhelming wave as the pressure is released. Stomping on the backfilled grave in my boots wouldn't be enough, and the jumping might disturb the lambs on the tombstones. I'd have to load the truck bed with rock or railroad ties and roll the rear tire back and forth over the cut space to reproduce a comparable pressure. But even this doesn't account for the coffin and the concrete vault's displacement in the hole. There is still too much dirt if the ground immediately after the burial is to look like a bed in which someone has just gotten up from a nap. And that's what it felt like—as though I was straightening the covers of my grandmother's bed after a nap. She must be somewhere in the house or in the yard tending the flowers. Digging the grave was an excavation of the depth of time I had spent with this woman, but there was nothing but dirt—no rocks, or scraggly roots, or pieces of glass from old pop bottles, or even earthworms. The dirt changed color after eight inches, going from gray to a drained red clay. Even my muscles were empty. No memories were released in the strain as I lifted shovelfuls of dirt onto the tarp. It felt like I was digging a hole for a tree or a dead cow. I measured the time and the daylight against the depth. I looked forward to lunch and kept digging. It may be that I wasn't excavating a buried city as Benjamin suggests but building one in an emptiness in which the hole and not the ground itself was the foundation for a city where I would be interred. The dirt was only a deposit. It was the pressure like an undertow that was let loose in the excavation that hides the treasures. I had been practicing for years to dig this hole. It was beautiful.

The deeper the eight-by-four-foot outline is sunk into the ground, the more difficult it is to keep the template true. The sides of the grave have to be sliced straight with the spade to keep it from rounding, which leaves the walls marked by the spade in a scallop pattern like the bottom of the ocean where there had been hundreds of moving shellfish. Near the statue of John Pelham at the cemetery entrance was a grave covered in bleached seashells. The homesickness was painful. The ocean is 350 miles away. The dirt on the tarp was smoothed and manicured into the shape of a beached whale. I finished the grave in the dark around 6:30, in the rain. I covered the dirt with another tarp to keep it dry. Scraped the mud from my tools and loaded them into the back of the pickup. In the bottom of the grave, the red clay was turning slick. In the night, its dark was another sea awaiting a body. Mary Pullen would not be buried here. She would see the grave I gave my mother's mother, Pearl Landers. A backhoe would dig Mary Pullen's grave years later.

Mary Pullen grew up in Boaz. Her father owned a hardware store. She went to a Methodist college in Montgomery, married AC, moved to Jacksonville and off the long, flat plateau called Sand Mountain. She had three children. She worked as the city librarian for over twenty years. There's a photograph of her and a small dedication hanging on the wall there now. Mary Pullen was the last of my grandparents. After AC she lived alone. Nothing changed about the house. It seemed to revolve on a hidden axis. And then everything shifted. Mary Pullen had a stroke in the midmorning working in the garden. She fell behind a stand of cosmos, her favorite flower, near the compost heap where the kitchen scraps were dumped. A cousin found her. He had come up to the house looking for lunch; otherwise it would have been hours later when Tommy Frost checked his cows. The beef cows were huddled against the barbed wire fence staring at Mary Pullen's crumpled-up body. She couldn't talk, but out of her came a low humming sound that sounded like a calf slumped in the grass. It was that sound that drew the herd to her. The stroke had left her paralyzed. But her eyes must have been as wide and wet as a cow's as my cousin picked her up in his arms and the flies spread into the air.

My mother called me. "Your grandmother has had a stroke," and very quickly she added, "She's okay. She's not about to die. She'll outlive me. The doctor doesn't know yet how extensive the damage is. You should go by the hospital and see her." I didn't cry. I believed my mother. I drove to the hospital and read to Mary Pullen from the Gospels. She loved that. I hugged her and left. I remember that she grabbed my face with her quivering hands and kissed me on the cheek, "I luvvv you, Allen." There was no need to cry. Afterward, she was confined to a wheelchair. Talking was very difficult. She would stammer and wave her hands like the cosmos drifting in a breeze. I started to practice her death. I sat uncomfortably across from her looking at her hands, counting the minutes. It was like being a deep-sea diver all alone in the dark water with no sensations other than those emanating from inside my own body. I had twelve minutes and no more before I would have to begin my ascent or get the bends, bubbling my own blood like the spit at the corner of her mouth. When she died it was as if only a small part of her had fallen off, like an old black toenail that had an iron dropped on it a couple of weeks back. Growing up, Mary Pullen used to tell me a story called "who stole my old black toe." In the story a woman is hoeing a turnip patch. She digs up an old black toe that has been whacked off. She takes it home and uses it to season her greens—cooking them so long the fat melts off the bone. That night in bed, half asleep, she hears a man coming through the garden and into the house looking for her, moaning, "Who stole my old black toe, who stole my old black toe?" I imagined the woman being dragged off to be eaten herself. No trace left except for a long mark in the dirt disappearing into the night.

The story isn't about feelings. That much I got as a kid, though I had no idea what the story was about. I hated greens. The story or at least a vestige of it has never left me. The account is about seasoning and how the dead flavor the living's world. The hunger of the living and the dead converge on a small piece of fat. The old black toe is a doorway to the supernatural stuck in the dirt, waiting to be uncovered by a hoe and dropped in a pot of simmering greens. Mary Pullen waits for me just beneath the dirt. My world would have no flavor without her. Mary Pullen lived five more years at a cost of $3,000 a month. To pay the bills the farm was timbered and sold off. I bought seventeen acres at market value from the estate. After she died, AC's dream mansion was sold to a chicken farmer. Mary Pullen was ninety-four years old. She outlived my mother by five months.

The Jurassic period of my life had to be when I lived under the care of Mary Pullen in an antebellum house just off the town square. The house was on a slight hill rising up from the street. The house looked even more imposing because of three enormous magnolias and a giant oak that slumbered in the front yard. A dilapidated picket fence set like a mouthful of teeth surrounded the front and sides of the house. There was a broad covered porch that wrapped around the house. There were two porch swings inside the vine-covered porch. I saw Abraham Lincoln's ghost standing in the corner of my bedroom next to the closet. Behind the kitchen was a room that must have been my father's room when he was a teenager in the early 1940s. There were pictures of military aircraft stuck to the wall with glue; some were hidden behind banks of murky Mason jars so that they appeared to be hanging behind clouds waiting for enemy aircraft. I was sure my grandfather had butchered two fat baby hippopotamuses in the cellar near the coal bin, though I never found any evidence of the crime. I would lie on the dining room floor on a faded Persian carpet underneath the massive dining room table—the shades and curtains were always shut so it was a perpetual dusk—looking at comic books about knights and Joan of Arc.

In this big house, I was never sure where my grandmother slept. Her dresser was next to a window adjacent to the room with the TV and my grandfather's rocking chair. I can see her looking in the mirror straightening her hat with the door to the porch directly behind her. Mary Pullen seemed to be a nomad in space. She was in the garden in the morning, at the TV for the show *As the World Turns,* and then at the library until four o'clock. She made a hamburger in a cast-iron skillet every day for me after work for a snack. Dinner in the kitchen just after dark, dominoes, a board game, maybe TV, and then she disappeared from my sight. AC slept upstairs in a room at the end of the hall. I slept upstairs in two different rooms depending on the night. My great-grandfather had a room downstairs next to the dining room before he was moved to a nursing home. Of all the rooms in the house, I have no memory of this space. It was a room that wasn't there. In my own bedroom I would let fireflies loose at night before I went to sleep. I would watch them float in a sky fourteen feet high.

At the heart of this world was Mary Pullen. She wasn't a great woman like Eleanor Roosevelt or beautiful like Eva Perón. She was round-shouldered with a plain face, and her hands smelled like green onions. At the library kids thought of her as their grandmother. For a short time there was a chance the new library would be named for her. It wasn't. The name was taken from an affluent donor. She was a member of clubs, like the garden club, the faculty club, Daughters of the American Revolution, and a devoted church member. At her death only a few of her connections were still viable. Her stroke was part of a five-year disappearing act until finally, in a futile gesture of showmanship, she was gone. There was one more appearance. At the funeral home she was washed. Her interior organs punctured. Her body pumped up with formaldehyde and rings placed on her fingers, rouge and powder on her face, and dressed in a gown to meet Jesus in; Mary Pullen was assembled for a cry and laid in her casket like a delectable treat. I loved Mary Pullen.

I had grown up in a town dedicated to remembering the dead from the Civil War. At the entrance to the city cemetery was the statue of John Pelham. Hundreds of dead soldiers were arranged in rows behind him as if they were massing for a charge on the strip mall across from where John Pelham stood. The city workers walked among the markers with weed eaters, barely noticing the fluttering plasticized flags. Pelham was matched in the center of town by the statue of a Confederate soldier staring north, his hands on a musket, the inscription on the base reading "men may change but values never do." Around the statue in a grid marking the points of the compass were large plaques set up like advertisements describing the generals from the area. Unlike the soldiers, they didn't so much die as transform into larger estates. Off to the side next to the waste can was a round slab of stone with a small iron plaque hammered onto the flat face describing the battlefield hospital and the number of men who died there. Just off the square in the Presbyterian church my great-great-uncle preached the mass funeral for the Confederate dead. My grandmother was still part of this service, which has now lasted over a hundred years. She was a member of the Daughters of the Confederacy. She wore a small ribbon with the face of General Forney stamped on a round piece of metal to the weekly meetings. The women remembered the dead. Her own death was supposed to be set in Confederate gray and wisteria like a small pearl. By the time Mary Pullen died the town had changed. The statue is still there, but the trees around it have been taken out. The generals' plaques are mixed now with street lamps that match the bank's decor. The Daughters of the Confederacy had been eclipsed by the Sons of the Confederacy, and fathers not mothers were invoked for remembering the ancient past. What was left of the old houses was bulldozed to make way for McDonald's, quick shops, and Kentucky Fried Chicken. On the site of the old funeral home, which had been a fraternity house and before that a remainder from the antebellum, a spanking new Hardee's was built, sealing off with a concrete slab all the blood washed into the groundwater beneath it and any evidence that there was ever anything else there.

Those years made a huge difference. Mary Pullen had outlived her time. Existing as a statue in a wheelchair propped up next to the TV set in the living room—set against her collection of Madonnas, she could be porcelain too. Her contemporaries were either dead or in nursing homes. When she did make it to church or the grocery store, she was treated like a magician doing a poor disappearing act—they just looked away. With her sequestration the town's structures, which had during the length of her life been dedicated to remembering the Civil War dead and by extension making everyone who could get into the city cemetery a piece of something bigger, came undone and dissolved into tiny bits.

I never suspected how easily she would disappear from my life. She had been stubborn. It wasn't like she fell through a trapdoor into a puff of smoke. She vanished in excruciatingly slow motion in plain view. I just couldn't watch it. Foucault captures her disappearance in a sentimental line that could have come from one of the historical romance novels she loved: "There were those who made something of the fact that a dog had lain the day before on the grass where fire had been, had been chased away several times, and had always returned. But it is not difficult to understand the animal found this place warmer than elsewhere."[1] A strange collage is made by placing the story of Damiens' execution and Mary Pullen together. Foucault's famous opening in *Discipline and Punish* showcases the regicide Damiens torn apart in a methodical, calculated execution. His pieces—a torso in the shape of a teardrop; a burned hand on a quartered arm, the other arm dangling from a bit of rope or leather; the two legs, thighs torn at the hip, skinny calves splattered with blood—are gathered up and placed on a pyre. There Damiens burned into dust. Foucault juxtaposes this scene against the portrait of a prison forty years in the future. There is no overt violence. The body isn't dispersed, but collected in concentrations of time, space, and discipline. Time is soaked into the individual's muscles and fat. Foucault's history of the prison via the body changes how my grandmother's death would normally be told. What draws me to the collage is the ending where the dog is lingering on the warm spot where Damiens had been burned into ashes. As the account matter-of-factly reports, "It is not difficult to understand the animal found this place warmer than elsewhere."[2] Thinking about my grandmother, I too am drawn again and again to her death, to that warm spot to try to rescue something, to finally get my feelings right, to answer Benjamin's assertion that "people who nothing moves or touches any longer are taught to cry again by film,"[3] and know at last why her death spot is warmer than other points in my life.

How the body is zoned and organized is the key to deciphering the emotional murk around Mary Pullen's death. Emotions are drawn out of the body as part of a larger configuration of making power. Foucault's proximity pushes the question of where the eyes are and how the tear does or does not erode the panopticon. I was amazed at how light she was in the casket as I lugged her up and down the aisle to the front of the church. She had already disappeared. The food was bad at the church fellowship hall. A man was dressed like he was going to a New Year's Eve party in an Italian, black, double-breasted suit. These were the mysteries. Mary Pullen wasn't assembled to make me cry. Others did, perhaps out of obligation or habit. My aunt sniffled discreetly off to the side. A fat relation choked back sobs graveside. I scanned the crowd as I rubbed my son's crewcut. The parts weren't right for me. I required a traditional graveside service. I looked blankly off into the distance. Emotions are part of an assemblage of machines like a possum running down an ironing board onto the foot of a man holding an electric fan in a steel washtub. It's me at the end. Mary Pullen is an assemblage—the liver spots on her hands, her tousled white hair, a certain smell, onions and perfume, slightly floral, a hoe in her hand, or a romance novel in large type, or a buttered corn muffin. This is only the closest layer, or field, of the assemblage. The layers go in increments—two inches, eight inches, and twelve inches, connecting the objects in the room, in the architecture, by the second or the minute, or even how she lingers in the room like the smell of greens boiling in an aluminum pot. The person is what Deleuze and Guattari describe as an assemblage of machines—body parts and objects combined to produce and monitor flows like spit, tears, milk, or honey slowly drooling out of a pitcher with a thumb slide.[4] Emotions are another flow, like the spit or the honey. The parts of the funeral would have to be fiddled with to get the appropriate flows from me. I refused to give the gesture. The open casket was the wrong connective tissue. Her body approached wax. The cemetery itself was wrongly situated; too close to the highway and the university coliseum to conjure up deep tears.

A flow is the connective tissue that ties one piece to another through a site. The architecture contextualizing these lines isn't just the four walls of the room or the force field surrounding the cemetery generated by the convenience store a quarter mile away—their business was good that day—the coliseum with its neon marquee, the trucks on the highway, and the student apartment building butted up against the cemetery. The architecture is the sunk-in structure that permeates relationships. Raymond Williams, in an attempt to trace the depth of hegemony, describes the orchestration of experience as structures of feeling.[5] He shies away from emotions himself, preferring the drier word "experience," but nevertheless the term "structures of feeling" attempts to articulate the interpenetration of hegemony in the individual. More closely, what constitutes hegemony here is the introjection of the commodity into the person and the relations of exchange into the emotional field. The tear is commodity-saturated liquid with the weight of mercury. The tear is Foucault's secret building block to the new prison he imagines. Emotions are displays and obfuscations of commodity fetishization.

Emotions are the connective tissue between the person surrounding the dead and the commodities that make up the event. The gift is as dead as Mary Pullen.

I did cry in the aftermath of the funeral. The connective tissue can run a long distance. I had to leave for the airport immediately after the funeral. My ten-year-old Tyree did to me what Mary Pullen's funeral couldn't. He wanted me to stay an extra day in Alabama. I needed to get back to Walla Walla, Washington. I had classes on Monday. He quit talking to me in the car. I sat in the front seat quietly crying. A single tear was worth $11.65. This was the practical cost of being a migrant professor. Death comes in small circles with the exponential increase in the distance Tyree was able to mimic in his silence, the removal of my grandmother, and the loneliness of doing sociology unconnected except telephonically to those I care about. People die far away.

That summer after my grandmother died I came to the cemetery to find her grave. At Christmas four months after her death there was not yet a stone marking her grave. I got lost hopping from one stretched-out clay outline to another trying to find my grandfather's stone. Now I had directions. The stone was in place. There was no grass over the grave. The red clay was outlined in Bermuda grass that was just starting to crack the surface with its rhizomes. It had been a dry spring and summer. Floating above where her kidneys might have been was a small fire ant mound like a whirlpool turned upside down. On the surface was the smallest tip. Beneath, the tunnels opened up like a tower made up of tiny passages reaching several feet down. This was only a small mound. It would have been beneath the blades of the tractors mowing the grass. The urn by the stone was on a hinge to make the mowing easier. It was just a matter of time before the grounds crew poisoned this colony. At the center of the graveyard was a statue of Jesus, kneeling with his arms opened so much like Bear Bryant, welcoming players into an afterlife in which Jesus himself was disappearing. He too was part of a lost world.

Almost never in all the talk about God and the Law is the simple law Jesus lived ever applied. Even preachers, especially preachers, get high and mighty and forget how simple the Gospel is. Love thy neighbor. Love is the great commandment. That's how he walked and lived. That's what he did every day. Pride gets in the way of people hearing this. People get fancy and want to show out. Walking around like they own the world and carried it in their pockets. But it's as simple as pie. All you gotta do is eat it. In whatever you're doing, whether you're sipping iced tea, digging a hole in the garden, stringing barbed wire in the pasture, cleaning the dishes in the kitchen, or watching the kids play, you're a sinner but Jesus still loves you. You can't change that basic fact on your own. That's the Law kicking in. But saved, the Beloved's blood covers you from head to toe and Jesus, and not you, carries the weight of the world. Suddenly you're as light as a feather and as strong as steel. *[At a few points, in all the immense literature devoted to Walter Benjamin, is this simple Proustian move applied—that in the most mundane act of sipping tea or the construction of a labyrinth of quotes, it is the beloved that lies on the material details like a heavy fog.]* You pick up a shovel or a dish towel and the whole universe moves if you're saved. Jesus covers everything you do. His blood is sweet as honey. (Preacher's name unknown; from a field recording I made on Sand Mountain)

Mary Pullen lived the last years of her life on the top of the hill overlooking two lakes, a red barn that had been a house in an earlier incarnation, and a patch of pine woods with chicken coops stashed underneath. These pines were some of the last to be timbered to pay her medical bills. Her world got much smaller. Her club friends were gone. A nurse stayed with her twenty-four hours a day. The house was unremarkable. The only extravagance was the fireplace. Mary Pullen hadn't burned a fire in years though. She still loved to watch *Jeopardy* and *Wheel of Fortune*. On special occasions she would be loaded up in the car and taken to the beauty parlor or the grocery store. Sometimes we would go to lunch at Big Daddy's Drive-in. On warm days the nurse would roll her out into the front yard. Mary Pullen would stare across the landscape toward the lake. Her eyes were fixed. Maybe she was daydreaming underneath the stare. I found out from the nurse that Mary Pullen had had a crush on Spencer Tracy ever since she was a young woman. The nurse rented every movie she could find with Spencer Tracy in it for her to watch. Mary Pullen had difficulty speaking now. The stroke had garbled her into a perpetual Pentecost. She listened, said my name, and touched my face with her hands. What she thought about looking out across the lake is a mystery that occurs to me now more than then. I was sitting across from Mary. I was holding my hand in my lap as if it were hers. She was wrapped in a blanket. I was kidding her about Spencer Tracy. She looked at me and smiled. A hummingbird suddenly appeared next to her head. Mary loved hummingbirds. The bird hovered right next to her ear beneath a tuft of white hair, just as if it were a bloom held still in a breeze. Then it was gone, appearing twenty yards away in an instant, unzipping a line in the air. Mary never saw the bird. She couldn't separate the beatings of its wings from the noise inside her head. It was then I realized how far Mary had gone. She had become like one of the complicated arrangements she did with her collection of porcelain Madonnas and flowers from the garden. I might as well have said look at the hummingbird to the blankets in the wheelchair. What I loved was a mark, a slight odor in the wool, a smudge on the aluminum wheels. Duchamp described these adhesions of the body on objects as the "infra-thin," but there is no hint of nostalgia or loss in his usage. The adhesion is momentary. The odor in the wool dissipates in an ordered chemical breakdown; the body's perfume molecules become unhinged from the blanket and the aluminum. The transfer of humanness and objectness is the flow beneath Duchamp's infra-thin that spawns a delicate bloom inches above the swamp like the woman at the heart of a complicated arrangement. Duchamp's temporal scale brings the question of how long my grandmother will stick to those objects saturated with her. This is another assemblage of Mary. Shortly after the hummingbird, my mother helped me acquire the kitchen table where I sat in Mary's kitchen as a kid. The table itself was nothing special. It was an old pine table, unpainted, two and a half by six feet. My grandmother didn't want it. She had few sentimentalities. It now sits in a warehouse in Alabama, waiting for me to take it north. There is a transfer happening. My grandmother is disappearing even in my memory, but she is simultaneously becoming the oceanic fog that clogs the pores of the table. After the funeral there was a mad rush to claim pieces from Mary's house. This was a full-scale raid. The house was stripped clean. Pieces that were not even my grandmother's were claimed. My mother's corner cabinet was loaded up in a truck. I got a syrup pitcher, a clear glass, fist-sized container with a thumb slide on the pour that had sat on the kitchen table for years. My wife secured this for me. For me it was the equivalent of having Marcel's tea set and a reminder that Mary Pullen loved me.

Proust's madeleine scene is part of a series of scenes and pieces within each scene, dedicated to the reclamation of memory and the emotional webworks of his childhood. Neither the syrup pitcher nor the madeleine is alone. This pivotal scene in Proust is produced not by one object but from the intersection at the recorded moment of a roomful. The madeleine may be the critical actant in Proust's account because of how easily the cook's hands from the narrator's childhood meld with the flour, butter, and sugar to become an active assemblage and are able to melt away in the mouth with the tea, or it becomes the critical actant in Proust's scene because of its proximity to the triggering of memories that fill Marcel. Any one of the objects there—his aunt's perfume, the smell of the cushions, the clinking of the spoons against the teacups, the afternoon light, the fixed arrangement of the furniture—all had a role and could have been the critical agent. There was a symphonic wave inside Marcel's head. There is no comparable scene in Benjamin's *A Berlin Childhood around 1900* or its ancestor "A Berlin Chronicle." The overwhelming emotion that fills Proust's pages like luxuriant vegetation and produces characters that are equally as luxuriant is matched in Benjamin's works with the barest hints of people, almost ghosts of ghosts, in a spatial, architectural recording. Grief doesn't well up in Benjamin. Grief is chronicled in a maze of spaces. In Proust what holds the memories in place is how the tastes and smells are linked with what Pierre Bourdieu called habitus—how the body is conditioned, flavored, configured around a map of social class that is anchored in fact and fantasy.[6] Benjamin extends the concept of habitus to the objects in the room and the room itself. In Benjamin's memory pieces, he isn't just recording how his memories reinscribe space; he is systematically building a series of drainage ditches to collect the humanness in commodity fetishism that culminates in an aqueduct laid like a memory palace on the swamp. What if the unfinished *Arcades Project* were an enormous waterworks waiting to be turned on to produce lakes made of tears?

Benjamin described Proust's thirteen-volume novel-memoir as a monumental effort to rescue memory from a world growing flatter and faster. It took thirteen volumes because of the Herculean effort needed to accomplish this. In another essay published in 1936 called "The Storyteller," Benjamin lamented the passing of the storyteller. What could this mean to a man who tried to tell stories with the recitation of architectural spaces and collected quotes arranged like objects in a gigantic living room? *The Arcades Project* was Benjamin's Herculean effort. It was Benjamin's attempt to create the equivalent of characters/subjects in a world superseded by objects and images becoming gigantic. Whereas Kafka and Proust emerge full-blown in Benjamin's writing, whenever he tried in his public writing to portray actors, they became ghosts in an ordered landscape. Only in something like his *Moscow Diary* does the grief and sadness produced in a broken love affair find expression in the bodies he portrays. Nevertheless, Benjamin looked homeward like his angel at the disasters mounting, even after home had passed away, and continued to labor on his aqueduct project.

Just off the corner of Mary Pullen's house, in full view of where she would fall after her stroke, was a four-by-five-foot brick outbuilding that housed the pump for the well. The bricks and roof matched the house, which made it look like a fancy outhouse. Stray tools were stacked inside. Plump black widow spiders were hidden like heartfelt valentines under the buckets. The structure was a cricket metropolis. The crickets would hop in all directions once the door was opened. The pump was electric. Big thunderstorms would knock

out the power and cut off the water supply for hours. AC never con-
jectured how large the aquifer was under the hill. He was concerned
with how deep the well had to be drilled. Each foot cost so much.
The body of water on which the house floated was never named or
thought about. It was the invisible body, a liquid ghost barely one
hundred feet underground. In front of the Big House where I lived
was an open well maybe thirty feet deep. Down the length like an in-
verted tower, handholds were squared into the wall at regular inter-
vals and acted as a ladder. At the bottom was a rim where the digger
must've stood over the circling dark water. Looking down I could
see my own face and occasionally a snake stretched out on the ledge.
The snake would look back at me. The sides were smoothed in the
same scallop pattern that marked Pearl's grave. The water was metal-
lic tasting and cold. Across the top of the well at ground level was a
square concrete form that was slightly larger than the hole and acted
as the ledge for the well basin and wooden winch. There were other
deserted wells scattered across AC's property that had pine boards
laid across the opening in the ground with no concrete ledge. These
were like mouths that had escaped braces and lay hidden like traps
under thickets of blackberries. These should have scared me, but it
was the thought of being buried alive by a cave-in while digging that
gnawed at me. I'd heard stories of these deaths. The walls sodden
with rainwater collapsing on the digger. As I was digging the final
foot of Pearl's grave in the cold light rain, this thought crossed my
mind more than once, which is why now as I remember it I am so far
down in a hole, looking out, shoveling the four-foot-deep grave. The
extra feet are intangible, pieces of the netherworld tethered to the
material world. They are part memory, part fantasy, part Edgar Allan
Poe, but real in the sense of what Benjamin meant by excavating the

past. Benjamin doesn't acknowledge the danger of a cave-in, of having the liquid in the dirt reach for you. At the bottom of the well is another sea and the ancient city filled with a treasure Benjamin described, but it isn't unguarded, and once the digger has started, and here Benjamin could be echoing Kafka, he "must not be afraid to return again and again to the same matter."[7] There is no stopping point, no single sheet of water to arrive at, but water like memory in endless sheets of mica to be peeled off layer by layer.

On the old map from the Confederate surveyor, what was my house was identified as the Widow Burton's. It's likely her husband, like so many others from the valley, died in the Civil War. Burton is the first name on the deed. After the widow died, there is a gap in the record of ownership and of who lived in the house until the Coppick family moved in. But it is unclear whether they were renters, were sharecroppers just biding their time, or owned the house. Sometime in the 1920s a man named Warlick bought the house. There is another gap until the late 1940s when A. C. Shelton bought the house and the 120 acres surrounding it. A hired hand, John Parker, moved in. He stayed until the great drought in the early 1970s lowered the well to the mud. He moved east across Highway 9 to a small house right on the road to Rabbittown. The Big House was empty. I used the backroom to store my bee equipment. The center of the house was rented by an artist who used it as a studio. He is a successful wildlife artist now. AC gave my wife and me the house and two and a half acres plus a $10,000 loan to restore it in 1978. We lived six months without water until the county finished a line that they had told us would take a few weeks. We sold the house in 2004 to a lawyer who planned on using the farm as a weekend getaway. It's an odd list: Burton the possible soldier, Coppick the sharecropper,

Warlick who hunted treasures and built the mule barn, John Parker the hired hand, the artist and the bees, and then me, a mixed-up time traveler who tried to bring the farm back. AC told me not to do it. "You can't pour your life and all your money into a piece of land." It doesn't remember. The lawyer has money. The pine trees I planted as a windbreak are still there, as are the walnuts I planted when AC died. The rocks from my dogs' graves have been relaid around flowers. Of all the owners I have traveled the farthest. Burton might have made it as far as Virginia maybe. The others died within miles of the house. I sit in Buffalo, New York. I wonder how I am like those other men who shared the same spaces, the shade of the pecan trees, and the sills of the house that date back to trees growing when de Soto pushed through. The same creek ran in the back. Crooked Mountain watched from the west. One thing that was different was that my relations lived on all sides. My mother and father's house was across the street a quarter mile away. AC and my grandmother's house was through the pasture on a hill no more than a half mile away. My uncle and his family lived just over a dip in the pasture from my grandparents. No other owner was as well entrenched. My wife's family was in town and farther east into the county. Like most of these men I was a hired hand. I worked on AC's farm and other farms down the road. But I was a time traveler looking back for a moment I can't describe except in the awkward word *home,* which is inseparable from Mary Pullen.

Proust's cookie, once in his saliva, expanded to the size of the lost world of his childhood with what could be called home as its capital. The yearning for this space inspired the meticulous recollection that Benjamin hints at in the opening quote taken from his own version of Proustian archaeology. For Proust and Benjamin, home is the mysterious city at the end of the excavation. Mary Pullen wanders its passageways in mine. Home is a projection into the future as well as backward. Nostalgia pulls in both directions. In a Borges short story the Minotaur dreams of a new home smaller, but no less a labyrinth, than the one he is trapped in. When he dies under Theseus's sword he barely resists because of the dream. His body twitched no more than the natural reluctance to feel the bronze blade slip across his throat and into his torso. The Minotaur doesn't dream of pastures or his childhood home—he never left it—but a smaller space. How much smaller? For Borges the answer could be infinitely smaller. What is left are memories as a simulation of space that are distorted and shrunken as when a vacuum forms inside a thin metal gas can. Thousands of mouths suck the outside in, leaving a distorted metal flower.

On either side of my grandmother's house were two lakes. They were called the Big Lake, which spread out into a mile-round circle, and the Little Lake. The lakes were fed by the same creek that ran behind my house. It sprang up at the bottom of Crooked Mountain and ran beside the blacktop until it emptied into a larger creek two miles down the road. In the nineteenth century the creek ran strong enough to power a mill. The grinding stone was still there in the 1940s. AC saw it. The mill, like the other old home places, fell back into the leaf litter and dirt. AC had a backhoe chop a small ditch through the pasture to fill the scraped-out bottom for the lakes and rigged a concrete rock dam with a board stuck into the gap to regulate the water flow into the lakes. Over time, the ditch clogged with silt and mud and spread out like an outstretched hand reaching for the water. Cattails and bulrushes were knit into the mud. I took a big digging hoe and opened up the channel slogging through the mud. This was the lake where the water moccasins were the thickest. Without ever seeing one in the marsh I imagined them there, the size of anacondas, sliding through the mud and grass, waiting to drag me to the bottom of the green water.

From the Little Lake the water spilled over a single-brick-wide dam through a three-foot ditch to an underground culvert that spewed the water across a low slope into the Big Lake. The lakes were stocked with bass and crappie and then grass carp and catfish. There were greenback turtles and forty-pound snapping turtles. Bullfrogs big enough to eat mice hunkered along the edges. This system was AC's great hydraulic achievement on the farm, an aquatic dream-world stocked with fish. The lakes were a new historical form. They didn't exist on the Confederate surveyor's map. There were beaver swamps where the springs overflowed. AC drained the swamps and turned them into pastures. Then he had lake bottoms constructed and water diverted and held in clay-bank storage units. In the beginning the cattle had access to the water and would wade out to stay cool in the summer. Barbed wire fences went up eventually. The lakes were stocked and fertilized. Public fishing was permitted for a small fee. On the new maps lakes dominate the landscape. They are liquid pyramids or, like the older wood-frame churches, an ideological form sheathed in a particular exoskeleton. Vinyl is the new skin for churches in the region. Commodity fetishism was the great unrecognized hydraulic achievement in the nineteenth century when whole rain forests of humanness were changed into deserts and deserts into giant subterranean lakes of humanness inside the commodity. Foucault chronicles the prehistory of commodity fetishization in *Discipline and Punish*. At Damiens' execution uncollected liquid is everywhere. The small liquids had not been stabilized into reservoirs of capital and discipline like those that turned the mills. There are puddles of muddy water, urine and shit thrown from the windows, sweat pools beneath the wool jackets of the soldiers, the saliva in the priest's kiss, the spit sputtering from Damiens' mouth, even the blood gushing from Damiens' thighs goes uncollected. The flow went into the ground. His tears were mixed with dust, but not in a combination that would create a new concrete. In a hundred years Foucault finds the concentrated tear of the child saint as he lay dying in Mettray Prison to be as solid as the stones in the wall. "What a pity I left the colony so soon."[8] Across the road AC built another two lakes. For a time the high lake was named Lake Mary Janie and a hand-painted sign was nailed to a tree. The name didn't stick. The lower lake wouldn't hold water year-round. A sinkhole opened up in the deepest part like a plug pulled inside a bathtub. The clay bottom was too thin and the underground pull too much, leaving a ten-foot-wide crater after sucking the water and the smaller fish away. The lake would fill up with the winter rains and then re-cede into nothing by July.

A dock was built on Little Lake. In the center of the water a wood and metal barrel raft was anchored for swimming. AC never swam, but Mary Pullen slid into the water like a seal. In the water she was transformed. On land she plodded. In the water she had an animal's grace. She would float effortlessly on her back with her arms and legs barely moving. Her swimsuit emphasized her tan arms and neck and creamy white shoulders. Her bones must have been as delicate as a frog's. Mary Pullen was round-shouldered and slightly humpbacked, but in the green water she had a whale's intelligence. The kingfishers that nested along the bank would streak across the lake's surface as if she were a turtle floating in the water and not a person. Mary Pullen drew all these animals into her person through her mouth. She ate everything. She was a dominant carnivore. She ate fried frog legs, turtle soup, poached guinea eggs, boiled poke salad, possum, and with gravy, raccoon, squirrels, rabbits, goat, chicken, and heifers from the farm. She was at the epicenter of widening rings of violence that reached out of her kitchen into the pasture. My grandmother, like the Virgin, watched over the slaughter of innocents and became after her stroke like those things that went into her mouth—consumable. Mary Pullen was generous with her money, even if the amounts were small—$100 here, $50 another time. At Christmas she gave $20 bills in white envelopes. She loaned me $20,000 to pay my mounting bills when my son Tyree was born. She supported another relation straight out. Money, food, board, everything was included. I watched him knock her and her wheelchair over in the front yard—his hands swinging over his head, yelling about more money. I grabbed my spade out of the truck bed. Mary Pullen lay there with a bewildered look on her face, the color of the blanket standing out against the grass. And then he walked off. I wondered if my grandmother would bob like a popper pulled under by a big bass. I could see my fat relation's white stomach like a bullfrog's gut standing out against the thin murkiness of the water as he pulled her ankle from below. From above her white hair would swirl and toss just beneath the surface moved by the gulps of air coming to the surface, leaving behind something like a photographic imprint in the water or the wavy pattern of a curtain being drawn shut. He baked a stray white cat in the back of my grandmother's green Impala for two days in the July heat. The temperature reached 120 degrees inside the Chevy. He opened the trunk expecting the cat to be dead or three-quarters dead, panting on its side. The cat was backed against the spare tire, hissing and spewing. He shut the trunk. He went inside the house and got a pair of fireplace gloves. Grabbed the cat and slammed it into an airline crate for shipping animals. He and his brother walked down the hill to the Little Lake, laughing. The big one had an eight-foot two-by-four under his arm. He slid the crate out into the green water. Took the two-by-four and pushed the crate underwater. The cat was white and stood out against the green water just like my nightmare of Mary Pullen's drowning.

> But of all the things I used to mimic, my favorite was the Chinese porcelain. A mottled crust overspread those vases, bowls, plates, and boxes, which, to be sure, were merely cheap export articles. I was nonetheless captivated by them, just as if I already knew the story which, after so many years, leads me back again to the work of the mummerehlen. The story comes from China, and tells of an old painter who invited friends to see his newest picture. This picture showed a park and a narrow footpath that ran along the stream and through a grove of trees, culminating at the door of a little cottage in the background. When the painter's friends, however, looked around for the painter, they saw that he was gone—that he was in the picture. There, he followed the little path that led to the door, paused before it quite still, turned, smiled, and disappeared through the narrow opening. In the same way, I too . . .[9]

It was August. The heat in the upper nineties reached down your throat like a snake crawling for a cool spot deep underground. The shade was listless except for the yellow jackets in their holes beneath the leaf litter. The pines stood still. The hardwoods were starting to shrivel. On some slopes off Crooked Mountain there were remnants of wild huckleberries and withered azaleas among scattered clusters of oakleaf hydrangeas. Here near the mouth to the highway, where there were the deepest piles of garbage and rubbish, the slopes were a desert prickled with catbrier and household appliances slowly burrowing into the ground. Early in the spring a Girl Scout troop had assembled here to sow wildflower seeds. The plan was to cover the garbage and the pushed-up red clay from the county bulldozers with a thicket of blooms, honeybees, and butterflies. It was a spectacular scheme that ended in complete failure. Nothing grew. The birds ate the seed, or they washed away in the torrential rains that came in May. The ground here was in the possession of a Spirit Queen whose world was that which was ruined. In a pile near the top of the mountain there was a dead hound with a steel choke collar. He clicked as hundreds of beetles cut passageways through his carcass. Nothing else was moving.

I paused and looked down the rutted road. To my left was a tiny fenced graveyard with two headstones clotted with rubbish and draped with bras and shredded underwear. On Christmas morning I saw a father and son standing together in this clearing on top of the mountain. Their Chevy truck was parked near an old refrigerator. Down a path were the graves of a husband and wife who ran a tavern on the mountain a hundred years ago. The boy was delicately fingering his new rifle. The father was next to him, pointing up into the trees. In a small pile next to their feet were two cardinals, a blue jay, and some darker gray-colored birds. I thought I could hear the birds singing through the creak of the rifle. "Good shot," the father said. It was clear they loved each other. "Keep your elbow straight. Squeeze the trigger."

The road had deep gullies woven into the clay. From the air it must have appeared as a desperate message coded into the dirt. I kicked off and imagined that I was a magnificent mountain bike rider, but I sucked. I was tired. There was no water in my bottles. My T-shirt was streaked with dirt. I picked my way down slowly, keeping my weight back and off the handlebars so I wouldn't cartwheel the bike if I buried the front tire in a hole. Coming around a slow curve I saw the Spirit Queen sitting in a brown vinyl La-Z-Boy recliner surrounded by ankle-deep garbage. I jammed on the brakes and stood V-legged in her presence. The world seemed to stop. No crows in the distance, no trucks on the highway, and the flies around the garbage paused. Inside the seconds there was a faraway electric shock coming for me. At the Queen's feet were three dead beavers laid in a particular pattern with their heads facing the Queen and their tails flattened out like they were obedient subjects. The corpses were brimming with maggots. And then she was gone. What was left was like a locust shell made up of individual pieces strung together and abandoned. What I saw disappeared in a set of stages like a kind of metamorphosis in reverse at high speed.

There was never anything there but the pieces. What I saw was like the poor man in Ambrose Bierce's short story "Occurrence at Owl Creek" who, before the rope grabbed his neck, saw a possible future where the rope breaks, he falls into the muddy water, and the soldiers miss him with their rifle fire. He makes it back home, and the instant he is about to hold his wife, the rope catches his weight and he sways back and forth off the bridge. In that full second he saw one future, perhaps even a glimpse into the afterlife. He also peered inside the desires of his own heart—a single beating part of what Darwin described as the tangled bank. "It is interesting to contemplate in the entangled bank, clothed with many plants of many kinds, with birds singing on the bushes, with various insects flitting about, and with worms crawling through the damp earth, and to reflect that these elaborately constructed forms, so different from each other, and dependent on each other in so complex a manner, have all been produced by laws acting around us."[10] But this bank's tangle was different. The assembly was as tall as six feet five inches, with broomsticks for legs stuck in high-top Nike basketball shoes with the laces untied. The torso was a rusted-out car muffler wrapped in a white terrycloth bathrobe. Where the heart would have been was a jagged cut in the metal as if a larva had eaten its way out. On top of the muffler's tailpipe was a dog's head in a bright red wig. The figure looked perfectly serene while the garbage vibrated with maggots and beetles. The arms rested on the chair; filling the sleeves were two long, stringy muscles made of wire. One hand was a brown cotton glove. The wire arm barely held up the weight of the cloth before the left arm opened into the clear flower of a broken beer bottle. What I saw was a vision into Crooked Mountain and my own future. I had seen Mary Pullen's skeleton pulled back from the future from where she slept in her grave and shown to me for an instant as her final blessing. It was a materialist supernatural outcropping, where commodity fetishism is linked to the ecosystem and new prophetic possibilities.

It is unfortunate that Marx didn't record the moment he arrived at the commodity as the elementary particle in the capitalist field and peered into it like it was Dorothy's Oz or Jean Cocteau's portrayal of the underworld just behind mirrors—a land, a whole geography as large as Alabama or Kublai Khan's empire just behind the thin membrane covering the commodity. Marcel Proust's character slipped across the threshold with the madeleine and tea and found himself in a world larger than the moment he was in—his childhood whose door was formed around a network of commodities.

Marx saw a demonic world filled with vampires and ghouls inside these same commodities. The insides of the commodity were as wretched and wicked as the factory slums he describes. Marx hides the labyrinth inside the commodity with his conceptualization of entangled labor and value, which on examination are as mysterious as transubstantiation. As I looked into the hyperworld left behind in the Spirit Queen's disappearance, it wasn't the long commodity trails stretching back in time and space from the individual commodities that pulled at me but the traces of Mary Pullen in the world that could be recovered under the care of her ghost. At the heart of the world Walter Benjamin describes in *Berlin Childhood around 1900* are his grandmother's apartment and postcard collection. The royal family is a diversion like the Minotaur in Daedalus's maze. It is the architect's torn heart that is the pattern for the labyrinth.

When I did come back two days later, the Queen's shell had been blown to bits with a shotgun, leaving big gaping holes in the easy chair. The torso was mangled, kicked down a gully next to a refrigerator. The hand was shattered. The broomsticks were splintered and stabbed in a pile of garbage. One basketball shoe was tossed out into the road. The other was unlocatable. In the chair in a heap were the wig and the bathrobe as if the Queen had been helped to disintegrate. I was alone in the woods. Above me was Crooked Mountain with a pine cross on its top. Above Benjamin was a picture of an angel.

Early in Walter Benjamin's career he acquired a Paul Klee print titled *Angelus Novus* in Munich. It is a relatively small watercolor and depicts a harpy-looking angel with an enormous head and eyes, finished with tiny outstretched wings. The angel appears to be a larva in a stage of abnormal development. Benjamin's longtime friend

Gershom Scholem described the angel as a clumsy-looking waiter trying to take an order. Klee's angel looked nothing like the pictures I saw in books at my grandmother's house—St. Michael appearing to Joan of Arc in the woods—or the angels cut into tombstones in the city cemetery. The angel hovered around Benjamin for a long time, waiting to take his order. It was one of his most prized possessions. On the eve of his first suicide attempt, Benjamin left the angel as a special gift to Gershom Scholem. This was July 1932. When he fled Paris in 1940, it was hanging in a large room at 10 rue Dombasle. Benjamin cut the print out of the frame and slid it into that suitcase stuffed with papers that made up *The Arcades Project*. He entrusted the suitcase to Georges Bataille. Here perhaps the angel found its home, looking over a paper city in ruins while Benjamin died looking over the ocean at the Spanish border. The angel stands back, cryptically out of reach, receding into the pages.

Kafka's narrator K. arrives in the village at dusk. Benjamin arrives at the first of several residences in Paris in 1930, now a permanent exile from Germany. Above the village, partially covered in clouds, K. glimpses the Castle. Benjamin begins work on his doomed *The Arcades Project*. It starts off as a small article for a journal and then fades into hundreds of pages with no end in sight. For the rest of the novel K. furtively tries to arrive at the front door before the chronicle just stops in midsentence, swallowed up by the same configuration of clouds that K. saw on the first evening. The gathering wreckage that nearly drowns Benjamin's Angel might as well have been the pages of his unfinished book. The closest glance K. gets of the interior of the Castle is the moment he steals into the official's carriage and falls asleep in the warm furs. He doesn't dream of home. Neither Benjamin's Angel nor K. looks backward into his memories.

Everything is directed toward the structure of the Castle and the construction of a memory palace waiting to be turned on. Zeno's paradox is endlessly repeated. Distance is interminable. Characters can't get in or, like Gregor or the mole, can't get out. Benjamin seems stuck like a beetle in amber. He moves with the speed of ooze. He won't leave Paris until the very last moment, and then it's nearly too late. Interiors and exteriors bend toward each other making it difficult if not impossible to distinguish them. Even without an insect's exoskeleton, Gregor is encased in multiple layers. On the mountains in Spain, Benjamin is lugging a heavy black suitcase. He lacks the swagger and grace of the flaneur. At one point he is so exhausted he is down on all fours drinking water from a puddle like a dog. K.'s zigzagging ends up a mimetic double of the Castle's interior in which there is no final resting point. Benjamin's suicide turns on the switch for his final project, which he never sees. He is the saint at the center of his paper Paris. At a few points in all the immense literature devoted to Walter Benjamin is the simple Proustian move applied— one of the most mundane acts, it is the beloved that lies on the material details. The consolation for Benjamin or K. or me is the mirage that haunts the Minotaur; the next labyrinth will fit more closely.

Notes

PREFACE

1. The individuals and some of the historical events are composites of ethnographic fiction and memories. See Walter Benjamin, "The Storyteller," in *Selected Writings*, vol. 3, *1935–1938*, ed. Howard Eiland and Michael W. Jennings (Cambridge, Mass.: Harvard University Press, 2002).

2. J. E. B. Stuart, *General Orders #9*, March 20, 1863, official records.

3. Walter Benjamin, *The Arcades Project*, trans. Howard Eiland and Kevin McLaughlin (Cambridge, Mass.: Harvard University Press, 1999).

4. Walter Benjamin, "A Berlin Chronicle," in *Selected Writings*, vol. 2, *1927–1934*, ed. Michael W. Jennings, Howard Eiland, and Gary Smith (Cambridge, Mass.: Harvard University Press, 1999), 598.

5. Walter Benjamin, *One-Way Street*, in *Selected Writings*, vol. 1, *1913–1926*, ed. Michael Bullock and Michael W. Jennings (Cambridge, Mass.: Harvard University Press, 1996), 447.

THE MARK ON THE SPADE

1. Fernand Braudel, *Civilization and Capitalism, 15th–18th Century*, vol. 2, *The Wheels of Commerce* (New York: Harper & Row, 1982), 459.

2. Bruno Latour, *We Have Never Been Modern* (Cambridge, Mass.: Harvard University Press, 1993), 6.

3. Manuel De Landa, *A Thousand Years of Nonlinear History* (New York: Zone Books, 1997), 60.

4. Sigmund Freud, *Civilization and Its Discontents* (New York: Anchor Books, 1961), 11.

5. Gilles Deleuze and Félix Guattari, *Anti-Oedipus: Capitalism and Schizophrenia,* trans. Robert Hurley et al. (Minneapolis: University of Minnesota Press, 1983), 1.

6. Loris and Margery Milne, *The National Audubon Society Field Guide to North American Insects and Spiders* (New York: Alfred A. Knopf, 1980), 530.

7. Erving Goffman, *Asylums* (New York: Anchor Books, 1961).

8. Seven years before the publication of *Civilization and Its Discontents,* a photograph of Freud is taken. He is seventy-one years old. The photographer is unnoteworthy. Freud is alone against a blank background, not exactly sitting or standing, but poised on the edge of movement like a praying mantis in a suit with a cigar in his hand. His jacket is open. He preferred a particular weave and texture, white shirt, bow tie. The hair and beard are meticulously groomed. He had them trimmed every day by a barber. Again, like some kind of insect, there is the snip-snip sound of the scissors just out of reach of the camera. Stepping back, there is a textural similarity between his beard and jacket. They are both cut thick and close, the weave responding like the hair or the hair like the wool. Beneath these details one can see that Freud's waist and torso are nearly equal in width. His biographer, Ernest Jones, puts it like this: "He had a strikingly well-shaped head, adorned with thick, dark, well-groomed hair, a handsome mustache, and a full pointed beard. He was about five feet eight inches tall, somewhat rotund—though probably his waist did not exceed his chest measurement—and he bore the marks of a sedentary profession." Ernest Jones, *The Life and Work of Sigmund Freud* (New York: Basic Books, 1953), 43.

9. It's not hard to picture what Jones means by these marks. Freud was fat by today's standards. His weight was settled like a big inner tube around his waist. What he doesn't say directly is that his hands were soft, his thigh muscles were

squishy, his butt was spreading, and that he was on the pale side. If what Jones doesn't say is pushed to a more invasive, closer level of detailing, other marks are visible. I think of a callus along his index finger from writing, his chronic constipation (reminiscent of Marx's hemorrhoids), a smudge on the page, an indentation in his leather chair or how a room smelled after he left. Or how a patient like Dora or the Wolf Man indelibly bore his mark after their short treatments. All these inscriptions are indicative of contact between bodies, objects, and a constellation of desire. The contact is not random but directive, organized to produce particular signs as markers. Freud dictates his own Ten Commandments on the bodies of his patients.

10. Jones isn't describing anything new here, nor did he mean to. He was pointing out sympathetically that Freud *looked* like he did because of *what* he did. In my imagination though, Freud's person looms up in his office like a big Rosetta stone, marked up, waiting for translation. Jones provides a history for the marks. They are evidence of a sedentary life. Freud didn't jog. The psychoanalysis he practiced revolved around sofas and chairs and not a schizophrenic's stroll. The differences are in calories. The schizophrenic had firmer thighs. The blank background in the photograph further frames Freud's sedentary movements. The blankness is an imaginary urban landscape filled with taxis, cafés, leather couches, books, museums, and office buildings. All around Freud objects are bustling, but Freud remains poised—not exactly moving or remaining still.

11. Jorge Luis Borges, *Other Inquisitions, 1937–1952* (Austin: University of Texas Press, 1984), 46.

12. Freud's work took place in this tight urban circle. His office and home were located in the fashionable ninth district of Vienna. His daily schedule included strolls along the boulevards and visits to the local cafés. His patients in the early years were predominantly residents of this same district and must have encountered Freud on the street. He would tip his fedora with a slight tilt of his head. He was always a proper gentleman. Perhaps it was on the strolls that Freud did his fieldwork for his book on jokes and their relationship to the unconscious. Instead of chasing butterflies, he collected pieces of conversation like

this infamous example: "A wife is like an umbrella, at worst one may take a cab." Freud reads the joke to be about the failure of monogamy. But the joke is implicitly about speeds—the speed of commodification or how fast is the cab or the gentleman with the umbrella masquerading as a wife moving. It is Freud's attempt to crystallize the speeds into a set jewel held with a gendered formation of the unconscious.

13. This background is imaginary because none of this is shown in the portrait. The background is blank like the fuzz across a TV screen, or a black cloth draped over a mirror. Behind this fuzz are other photographs that place Freud in settings outside of the café scene in Vienna. While not an athlete, Freud was apparently a powerful walker. Perhaps I should add a blister to the list of marks. In a photograph taken in 1913 in the Dolomites, Freud stands next to Anna looking like a prehistoric model for Banana Republic. He is still tightly dressed. His English boots are visible, fedora on his head, tweed suit, still the gentleman. Freud stands there like a parody of the painting *American Gothic* done with the TV character Oliver Wendell Douglas dressed in a suit with a pitchfork, Hungarian wife in hand, in the opening credits of *Green Acres*. Freud's urbane style is more than a fashion statement; it is the source of his organizing motifs. Throughout his work Freud's metaphors are relentlessly urban, as are his markings. Both are crucial to how Freud organized and prepared his materials. He was a species of landscaper. Under his hands the unconscious became a new architectural form, like the invention and cultivation of shrub mazes at Versailles. In the marks a royal will took form.

14. Steven Dubin, "Symbolic Slavery: Black Representations in Popular Culture," *Social Problems* 34, no. 2 (April 1987): 123.

15. During the surrealist heyday in Paris, the German refugee Walter Benjamin clarifies what I mean by a new architectural form. Benjamin describes the optical unconscious as the hidden world made accessible through new mimetic technologies. The camera as an eye can see details that were previously inaccessible. The shutter could freeze and isolate details that the eye couldn't get at. The new technologies materialize what could only be imagined before as the shape of a

drip of milk as it hits the forehead or how cancer spreads through a lung. Benjamin piggybacks his concept to Freud's unconscious with a critical difference. He adds a technological connection. The new world is intimately related to the presence of a machine. Freud is slow on this point. The dreamscapes he charts are landscapes constructed from words composed into rhetorical patterns. The unconscious is a prepared landscape made from actual contact with assemblages.

16. The preparation of the unconscious isn't limited to words. They may be the least important aspect, just another layer or imaginary surface to make into a circulating script. Freud's own construction—how tightly his tie was snugged around his neck, the thickness of his belt, where his socks were threadbare, whose hands ironed his pants—is an integral part of his self-fashioning as a Viennese gentleman and how such markings came into play in his case studies. In the case of Dora, it was a bit of jewelry she was fiddling with that gave Freud the opportunity to move his discussion of a dream image, a jewel box, out into the open and into Dora's hands, so to speak. Here the preparation of Dora as a feminine landscape and the slip points in that landscape, how her person fit her body and the objects were critical bands of evidence for Freud. Turning the same insights back onto him is problematic as multiplicities really start to swarm. Second, such mundane acts or features as whose hands ironed his pants point to a division of labor and economies, both essential to the construction of the unconscious. Freud's own writing on Dora bears this out, as one of the major sticking points in the case is who is working for whom. Dora, Freud, and Dora's father all work the class-servant metaphor back and forth with great effect and pain. Even Dora's suitor Herr K. plays the same class card in attempting to seduce Dora, using the same words with which he seduced the governess. Freud's person is just one layer in this system. His office functioned as a cue card for the patients. Stuffed with antiquities from Greece, Rome, and Egypt, "It was the smallish object, judging by the place left empty, my end of the semicircle, made by the symmetrical arrangement of the Gods on his table. 'This is my favorite,' he said. He held the object toward me. I took it in my hand. It was a little bronze statue, helmeted, clothed to the foot in carved robe with the upper incised chiton or peplum. One hand was extended as if holding a staff or rod. 'She is perfect,' he said, 'only she

has lost her spear.' I did not say anything. He knew that I loved Greece. He knew that I loved Hellas. I stood looking at Pallas Athene, she whose winged attribute was Nike, Victory, or she stood wingless, Nike A-pteros in the old days, in the little temple to your right as you climb the steps to the Propylaea on the Acropolis at Athens. He too had climbed the steps once, he had told me, for the briefest survey of the glory that was Greece. Nike A-pteros, she was called, the Wingless Victory, for Victory could never, would never fly away from Athens." Hilda Doolittle, *Tribute to Freud* (New York: New Direction Books, 1956), 68–69.

Freud re-created the classical world. The colonial third world was not there. There was no Africa, Brazil, or America. The absence of the third world is remarkable when compared to other revolutionary studios at the beginning of the twentieth century. Picasso's studio in Paris at the same time was filled with African masks and artifacts from around the world. For Freud, the new third world doesn't exist except in the residues of cocaine and the mention of a chocolate bar in a dream or in the dust that covers his office like the fog coming off the Niger in Conrad's *Heart of Darkness*. Add these elements into the scheme and the part the proper Viennese landscape played in ordering the mapping of the unconscious is exposed. Freud was a part of that landscape in what he experienced, how he was dressed, and how he marked his patients. Rearrange his marks and Freud himself is uncovered as another landscape, another layer of marking. Place the maid, the invisible secretary, or the patient into the scene and the office is further transformed. It is like the living room in Poe's "Tell-Tale Heart" where a body is hooked up to the house. The heart powers up the grandfather clocks and keeps time on the policemen's pocket watches.

17. Freud himself was an integral part of the Viennese landscape, not just in what he expressed, but in how he was marked, put together, dressed. Rearrange his marks, and Freud as a landscape mutates into something else altogether. Treat Freud like a paper doll and dress him in overalls, half boots, and a washed-out work shirt opened at the neck with rolled-up sleeves. Lose the facial hair to stubble, shorten the cigar. Put him on a sharecropper's plot in Alabama, sitting on the steps. Now the photographer develops. It is Walker Evans. But why stop here? Freud is drinking a Coke. Rewrite Dora as a sharecropper's daughter dressed in

a flour sack. Worms are as big a problem as the oedipal complex. Imagine a floral psychoanalysis instead of the dusty, antiquity-filled world Freud envisioned. If Freud had looked to the American South, or Brazil, for the framework of the unconscious, the oedipal complex might have had more rhythm, more Tara, more worms. This would have been a real civil war, a real oedipal Holocaust.

18. Freud, *Civilization and Its Discontents,* 17.

19. Ibid., 16–17.

20. Sigmund Freud, *Collected Papers* (New York: Basic Books, 1959), 5: 177.

21. Deleuze and Guattari echo similar sentiments in their opening to *Anti-Oedipus:* "A schizophrenic out for a walk is a better model than a neurotic lying on the analyst's couch." I have no problem with the stroll. Movement is critical. It's the view I want to rearrange. I want to take it off the street and into the country. Freud's contemporary, Kafka, sent K. to Oklahoma. I'd like Freud to go to Alabama with Walker Evans and James Agee to restock his dreamworld with pieces from an alien landscape. Freud did come to America in the first decade of the twentieth century to give a series of lectures at Clark University. He was not particularly enamored with the prospect of the trip: "The thought of America does not matter to me but I'm looking forward very much to our journey together," referring to his companion and disciple, Sandor Ferenczi. And then he added, "All I want to see is Niagara Falls." He saw Niagara Falls on September 13, which he found even grander and larger than he had expected. His feelings were hurt by a guide pushing the other visitors back and yelling, "Let the old fellow go first." He was fifty-three years old. From the falls, Freud took the train to a cabin in the Adirondacks near Lake Placid. They stayed for four days. Freud's sleep was disturbed by the frogs and a mild attack of appendicitis. It was here that he apparently wrote a letter to Elizabeth Hubbard, encouraging her in her studies and expressing pleasure at having met her. This is based on an entry in Elizabeth Hubbard's diary. Near the end of his stay he saw a wild porcupine, which became the inspiration for the phrase "to find one's porcupine." It was right after this trip that Freud worked on the first preliminary sketches of material that would appear in final form twenty years later in *Civilization and Its Discontents*. He had read

Charles Darwin's *Origin of Species* and was moved by the imagery in this passage. He was struggling with how to work out the persistence of the past in the unconscious in a naturalized architecture like one he had seen in a drawing from Ohio of a burial mound in the shape of an enormous snake swallowing an egg. His early work on the gonads of eels and the nervous system of crayfish may have prepared the way for this move toward an ecological psychoanalysis. But it proved unworkable. Instead, he produced the beautiful but sterile portrait of the unconscious as the city of Rome. Freud mineralized the unconscious. The streets of his Rome are deserted. There aren't any ghosts. No feral cats or rats. It's all marble.

What he did bring back from America was a small scar on his left calf at the flea bite line just above his garter from scratching. Freud broke out in a rash just after being bitten by fleas. It had been a particularly hot spring and summer in Worcester, which provided the perfect conditions for a flea infestation. The house he was staying at was the home of several dogs and cats that wandered the neighborhood at will. This was not the end of Freud's encounters with insects. Several patients, including H. D., noted small red bites after some of their sessions. Freud's chows Lin Yaj and Jo Fi suffered from occasional fleas. The dogs would lie at the foot of the couch during the analytical hour. In the middle of Freud's office packed with marble figurines and skeletons, another exoskeleton was burrowing into his patients under the silent gaze of Freud's marble dreamworld.

22. Walter Benjamin, *Illuminations* (New York: Schocken Books, 1969), 236–37.

THE ABDUCTION OF MARY JANIE

1. Walter Benjamin, *One-Way Street,* in *Selected Writings,* vol. 1, *1913–1926,* ed. Michael Bullock and Michael W. Jennings (Cambridge, Mass.: Harvard University Press, 1996), 445.

2. Jorge Luis Borges, "Coleridge's Flower," in *Selected Non-fictions,* ed. Elliot Weinberger, trans. Esther Allen et al. (New York: Penguin Books, 1999), 241–42.

3. C. Wright Mills, "The Promise," in *The Sociological Imagination* (New York: Oxford University Press, 1989), 3.

4. W. G. Sebald, *The Rings of Saturn,* trans. Michael Hulse (New York: New Directions, 1999), 17–18.

5. Max Weber, *The Protestant Ethic and the "Spirit" of Capitalism and Other Writings,* trans. Peter Baehr and Gordon C. Wells (New York: Penguin Books, 2002).

6. Max Weber, *The Protestant Ethic and the Spirit of Capitalism,* trans. Talcott Parsons (New York: Charles Scribner's Sons, 1958).

7. Thomas Osborne, review of Siegfried Kracauer's *The Mass Ornament, Times Literary Supplement,* June 14, 1996.

8. Walter Benjamin, *The Arcades Project,* trans. Howard Eiland and Kevin McLaughlin (Cambridge, Mass.: Harvard University Press, 1999), 872.

9. Walter Benjamin, *Moscow Diary,* trans. Richard Sieburth (Cambridge, Mass.: Harvard University Press, 1986), 121.

PLANCHETTE, MY LOVE

1. Walter Benjamin's collage project in his unfinished *Arcades Project* was designed to make pieces of text into an explosive combination that would send shock waves back into the past and cause the present to flit by like it was a dream that could be momentarily grabbed. The collages were miniature memory palaces collected into an empire that could go bang. As far as I know, Benjamin's juxtapositions were solely parts of historical texts. He doesn't take the next step as a ventriloquist and play with representation by adding fictive lines that would mimic and explode the original voice, making him a storyteller like his own essay by the same name. Take these almost scriptural lines from Marx: "A commodity appears at first sight an extremely obvious, trivial thing. Its analysis brings out that it is a very strange thing, abounding in metaphysical subtleties and theological niceties." Add to the Marx quote, in restless italics, and as if he had written them: *"But it is only one commodity, one bar of iron, one coat, one pair of shoes, or one bundle of linen in a network of commodities. Once these queer things begin to assemble themselves into stocks and displays in department stores, the devilment*

exponentially increases, even if at the center a single commodity acts as the queen." Creating this collage: "A commodity appears at first sight an extremely obvious, trivial thing. Its analysis brings out that it is a very strange thing, abounding in metaphysical subtleties and theological niceties. *But it is only one commodity, one bar of iron, one coat, one pair of shoes, or one bundle of linen in a network of commodities. Once these queer things begin to assemble themselves into stocks and displays in department stores, the devilment exponentially increases, even if at the center a single commodity acts as the queen."* A draft passage from *Capital* by Karl Marx, quoted in a version of H. G. Wells's *Outline of History.*

Then tell this story. The first lines are taken from the opening chapter of *Capital.* The second and third lines are deleted lines that were recovered by Wells from a notebook that Marx may have used to experiment with automatic writing in his construction of *Capital.* The notebook, Wells decided, was not credible, and he deleted the lines from his commentary on Marx. His deletion was discovered by Jorge Luis Borges in an encyclopedia on the occult published in 1898 under the entry *planchette.* The deleted lines would have added an important historical gloss to Marx's archaeology of the commodity. *Capital* was published in 1867, but Marx only partially grasped what the department store would do in the rest of the nineteenth and through the twentieth centuries in accelerating the effects of commodification and commodity fetishization. The deleted lines point to the future that *Capital* was metamorphosing into. Walter Benjamin would see more of these effects in his *Arcades Project* in the 1930s. But neither of them could foresee the rise of the supercommodity in the personalized brand name and the devastating power of commodity signage in everyday life. Even Marx melts into this thin air, Smithy into the deep lake on top of the mountain.

2. Michael Taussig, *Shamanism, Colonialism, and the Wild Man: A Study in Terror and Healing* (Chicago: University of Chicago Press, 1987).

3. Max Weber, *The Protestant Ethic and the "Spirit" of Capitalism and Other Writings,* trans. Peter Baehr and Gordon C. Wells (New York: Penguin Books, 2002).

4. Manuel De Landa, *A Thousand Years of Nonlinear History* (New York: Zone Books, 1997).

5. Despite its size, this elegant woodpecker is adept at keeping out of sight. Obtaining a close view of one usually requires careful stalking. Although primarily a forest bird, the "logcock" has recently become adapted to civilization and has become relatively numerous even on the outskirts of large cities, where its presence is most easily detected by its loud, ringing call and by its large, characteristically rectangular excavations in trees.

6. The new translation of Max Weber's *The Protestant Ethic and the Spirit of Capitalism* (trans. Stephen Kalberg, Los Angeles: Roxbury Publishing, 2001) reverses Talcott Parsons's boxlike rendering of Weber's prose from the iron cage to a more social psychological understanding of the modern individual. Apparently, Parsons's translation was driven in part by intradepartmental struggles with P. Sorkin.

7. Technically, *pH* stands for hydrogen ion concentration and is the measure or scale used to indicate the degree of acidity or alkalinity of the soil, of water, or of other media. Neutral is 7.0; lower values indicate acidity, and higher values alkalinity. The scale is in fact a logarithmic one, so that the difference between pH 7.0 and 8.0 is far greater than that between steps in the acid range, e.g., pH 5.0 to 6.0.

8. For this reason, the emergence of ecosystems is typically described as a succession of plant assemblages that interact with each other, passing through several stable states until they reach a "climax." A temperate forest, of the type that characterizes the European continent, for example, begins as an assemblage of lichen and moss, followed by scrubby birch and aspen, then pine forest, and finally a mature oak, lime, elm, and beech forest. Although it may appear otherwise, this process of succession does not have the climax state as a goal. Rather, the emergence of the ecosystems is a blind groping from stable state to stable state in which each plant assemblage creates the conditions that stabilize the next one. A variety of historical constraints (energetic, material, dynamic) determines at some point that there is no other stable state attainable from the current one, and so the process climaxes. This is, of course, just another example of the meshwork of heterogeneous elements evolving by drift. A more realistic model of this meshwork would have to include microorganisms, the myriad of insects and other

small animals that play key roles in the flow of biomass, and some decorative large predators, like tigers, wolves, or early humans. Manuel De Landa, *A Thousand Years of Nonlinear History,* 105–6.

9. Karl Marx, *Capital* (New York: Vintage Books, 1977), 1: 304.

10. "When we look at the plants and bushes clothing an entangled bank, we are tempted to attribute their proportional numbers and kinds to what we call chance. But how false a view is this! Everyone has heard that when an American forest is cut down, a very different vegetation springs up; it has been observed that the trees now growing on the ancient Indian mounds, in the Southern United States, display the same beautiful diversity and proportion of kinds as in the surrounding virgin forests. What a struggle between the several kinds of trees must have gone on during long centuries, each annually scattering its seeds by the thousand; what war between insect and insect—between insects, snails, and other animals with birds and beasts of prey—all striving to increase, and all feeding on each other or on the trees or their seeds and seedlings, or on the other plants that first clothed the ground and thus checked the growth of the trees! Throw up a handful of feathers, and all fall to the ground according to definite laws; but how simple is this problem compared to the action and reaction of the innumerable plants and animals that have determined, over the course of centuries, the proportional numbers and kinds of trees now growing on the old Indian ruins!" Charles Darwin, *The Origin of Species* (New York: Penguin Books, 1985), 126.

11. This was in late August. By October I was hacking up blood and mucus in the middle of the night. Any physical exertion sent me into convulsions. I had to give up training. No more running. The doctor told me I had chronic asthmatic bronchitis. I'd better move out of my house immediately. This was a sensitive subject. I had become a Christian early that summer after praying with a couple in their trailer. I was embarrassed and put off when they asked me to pray for revelation from God. "Oh," I said. "I believe in cramps from running marathons so give me a spiritual cramp." Thirty seconds later I had collapsed on the floor balled up in a knot. I couldn't speak. My hands were locked in fists. Legs were

paralyzed. This lasted for twenty minutes. I was never afraid. I wondered what they would say to the ambulance driver. We were praying and he had a fit? This was how my conversion happened. This attack of asthmatic bronchitis was interpreted by the local charismatic community as the Devil trying to steal my faith while I was still young in God's Word. Buried inside was the idea that God preferred property owners to renters.

12. Marx, *Capital*, 1: 176–77.

13. "Planchette (plan-shet: 9) N. [f., dim. of planche plank] A small board supported on castors and a vertical pencil, said, when lightly touched by fingers, to move of itself, the pencil thereby tracing words." *Webster's Secondary-School Dictionary* (Springfield, Mo.: G. & C. Merriam Co., 1913).

14. After first meeting Fain, I told my then wife, "That man is crazy." I used to run with his son Gus, a gawky, self-conscious nineteen-year-old. I'd come over to the house to get Gus to go for a run. I met Fain sitting in the kitchen. He looked like a bear crossed with Charlie Manson.

I was standing in the kitchen that opened into the next room, kind of a sitting area. The TV was minimal. There were two matching leather chairs and a sofa sitting on a large Persian rug. There were knives in droves spread across the walls in fan patterns. Big gut-sticking Bowies, pocketknives of all sizes, fish knives, skinners with carved bone handles, and a cavalry saber that Fain swore had been stuck through a soldier at Bull Run. Two shotguns faced each other like a couple in therapy. "They're Italian," Fain said. Over the mantel was a print housed in an elaborate frame, three feet by four feet, in which a stag was being ripped apart by a pack of Irish wolfhounds. In the kitchen Fain flipped back the lid of a pizza box and tore into the slices. His mouth poked out from his beard. A bottle of beer was on his right. "Gus," he roared. No answer.

That was the beginning. I was a critical element in bringing Fain to Jesus. It was a story I told him about a man with a hole in his heart who had tried to fill it with possessions that pushed him toward a conversion outside his condominium in Destin, Florida. Fain had a hole in his heart.

15. "There is a variety of gifts but always the same spirit; there are all sorts of service to be done, but always to the same Lord; working in all sorts of different ways in different people. It is the same God who is working in all of them. The particular way in which the Spirit is given to each person is for a good purpose. One may have the gift of preaching with wisdom given him by the Spirit; another may have the gift of faith given by the same Spirit; another again the gift of healing, through this one Spirit; one power of miracles; another prophecy; another the gift of recognizing spirits; another the gift of tongues, and another the ability to interpret them. All these are the work of one in the same Spirit, who distributes different gifts to different people just as he chooses." I Corinthians 12:4–11.

16. Before the Fluids arrived in person, their pastoral newsletter preceded them. Copies were available in the front of the church and tacked up on the bulletin board. What caught my attention was a message from George who had found the physical location of Heaven. Heaven was north or up from Alpha Centauri. In his exegesis there was no mention in the scripture for that star; instead, George relied on complicated, astrological-like grids to arrive at the most normally recognized star by name. But why imagine that Heaven was a physical place inside the same ocean of space as America? George followed Jesus' trajectory in the Book of Acts where he rises like a rocket into the sky and disappears from view. "As he said this he was lifted up while they looked on, and a cloud took him from their sight. They were still staring into the sky when suddenly two men in white were standing near them and they said, why are you men from Galilee standing here looking into the sky? Jesus who has been taken up from you into heaven, the same Jesus will come back in the same way as you have seen him go there." Acts 1:9–11.

This wasn't the cutting part of the newsletter. The edge came in the vicious anti-Catholicism. I was particularly sensitive to this because I used the Catholic Bible—the Jerusalem translation—and had strong ties with the local Catholic charismatic community. Even without meeting each other, we were on each other's hit list.

17. SHELTON: Fain, can you tell me why you thought I needed to be brought up for prayer?

EDWARDS: You're too prissy about your faith. You don't bite into the word of God. You stand back and look. You're so blessed but won't commit. You're scared of serving God.

SHELTON: I wasn't scared. I was more worried about hurting people's feelings if they saw my notebook. I didn't think they could read it, but it would be awkward trying to explain what I was writing.

EDWARDS: Explain what?

SHELTON: That the Fluids were false prophets. Liars. They're not from God.

EDWARDS: You reject God at every critical moment. You choose your books over Jesus.

SHELTON: You're wrong Fain. I . . .

EDWARDS: No, you're outside the blood of Christ.

18. The German refugee scholar Walter Benjamin captured the moment in his sample of a physicist's text. To Benjamin add snakes, a dead grandmother, and mice to mire the exhilarating speed. Instead, locate the disintegration of speed in mimetic excess in a haunting thick as honey.

> I am standing on the threshold about to enter a room. It is a complicated business. In the first place I must shove against an atmosphere pressing with a force of fourteen pounds on every square inch of my body. I must make sure of landing on a plank traveling at twenty miles a second round the sun—a fraction of a second too early or too late, the plank would be miles away. I must do this whilst hanging from a round planet head outward into space, and with a wind of aether blowing at no one knows how many miles a second through every interstice of my body. The plank has no solidity of substance. To step on it is like stepping on a swarm of flies. Shall I not slip through? No, if I make the venture one of the flies hits me and gives a boost up again; I fall again and am knocked upwards by another fly; and so on. I may hope that the net result will be that I remain about steady; but if unfortunately I should slip through the floor or be boosted too violently up

to the ceiling, the occurrence would be, not a violation of the laws of Nature, but a rare coincidence.

Walter Benjamin, *Some Reflections on Kafka,* in *Illuminations* (New York: Schocken Books, 1969), 141–42.

19. Smithy was uneducated. He was a big man who loved cornbread and buttermilk. He was from the hills of Kentucky, served in the Army, and became a Holiness preacher. Near the end of his career in that church, he must have been nearly sixty, he became convinced that the gifts of the Spirit were real and that we were in the midst of a new awakening during the last days before Christ returned. It was his vision and character that made Faith Temple.

20. At one service Smithy took a sermon from Genesis and the two curses laid on Adam and Eve for their transgressions. Once saved, a reversal was supposed to set in, he said. Pain should progressively disappear from childbirth. For the man, work didn't go away. Instead they had absolute dominion over the animals with their voice. Smithy recounted how he confronted his big bull and commanded him to obey. The congregation sat as quietly as the grass under Smithy's feet. "In God's name I command you to stop," he said. The bull supposedly stopped.

21. "Finally, grow strong in the Lord, with the strength of his power. Put God's armor on so as to be able to resist the Devil's tactics. For it is not against human enemies that we have to struggle, but against the Sovereignties and the Powers who originate the darkness in this world, the spiritual army of evil in the heavens. That is why you must rely on God's armor, or you will not be able to put up any resistance when the worst happens, or have enough resources to hold your ground." Ephesians 6:10–13. This passage was often quoted at church. For the congregation, everyday life was war. Backed-up toilets, financial problems, illness were all the result of the Devil's attacks.

22. Marx, *Capital,* 1: 164.

23. The act was assigned specific gender roles. Men always caught. In part the ritual was a reenactment of the conceptualization of Christ as the husband and the church as the bride. The scriptural references are multiple. The most famous

and difficult to completely domesticate is the erotic Song of Solomon. A safer passage is: "Then John's disciples came to him and said, 'Why is it that we and the Pharisees fast, but your disciples do not?' Jesus replied, 'Surely the bridegroom's attendants would never think of mourning as long as the bridegroom is still with them? But the time will come for a bridegroom to be taken away from them, and then they will fast.'" Matthew 9:14–15.

24. This is called being slain in the spirit or resting in the spirit. The only scriptural reference I am aware of is what happened when Saul encountered the risen Christ on the road to Damascus: "Suddenly, while he was traveling to Damascus and just before he reached the city, there came a light from heaven all around him. He fell to the ground, and then he heard a voice saying 'Saul, Saul why are you persecuting me?' 'Who are you Lord?' he asked, and the voice answered, 'I am Jesus, and you are persecuting me. Get up now and go into the city, and you will be told what you have to do.' The men traveling with Saul stood there speechless, for though they heard the voice they could see no one. Then Saul got up from the ground, but even with his eyes wide-open he could see nothing at all and they had to lead him into Damascus by the hand. For three days he was without his sight and took neither food nor drink." Acts 9:3–9. For most it is not nearly so dramatic. It is more a matter of letting go like a diver poised at the edge of the high dive. There is a correct form that facilitates the event. The individual stands straight, legs shoulder width as if at attention, hands clasped in front or down at the side. The stance should not change as the preacher steps in close and delicately slaps the forehead. Here is the test of faith, to fall backward off the heels into someone's arms. It is not really a trance. You hear everything around you. Time passes more slowly because of your awareness. At Faith Temple individuals would be down between thirty seconds and four minutes, with one minute being the average. It is a peculiar sensation to be lying on your back in church. It is as if you had completed a difficult dance step in front of an audience.

25. What is astonishing is not that I had a demon but that I had only one and that the demon was the demon of unbelief, which must have been an extremely large or efficient demon to cover such a large and expansive territory. The way she said it is that for every sin there is a single demon. The division of labor that character-

izes most large-scale bureaucracies is absent in Satan's kingdom. This explanation was repeated in other interviews in an ABC documentary that captured an exorcism in which a fourteen-year-old girl was inhabited by a demon from Africa, what I call a continental demon. The demon was not from any particular country or city, though the young girl did stipulate he was from the jungle. What also emerged from my conversation with Clarice is that the demon of unbelief entered me through my reading of sociology books.

26. Natalie Davis, *The Return of Martin Guerre* (Cambridge, Mass.: Harvard University Press, 1983).

27. Dan Rose, "The Landscape of Active Ingredients and Public Writing," unpublished manuscript, 1994.

28. Speaking in tongues is one of the gifts of the Spirit. The first reference in scriptures is "When Pentecost day came round, they had all met in one room, when suddenly they heard what sounded like a powerful wind from heaven, the noise of which filled the entire house in which they were sitting; and something appeared to them that seemed like tongues of fire; these separating came to rest on the head of each of them. They were all filled with the Holy Spirit, and began to speak foreign languages as the spirit gave them gift of speech." Acts 2:1–4. I never saw anything like this in the fourteen years I was involved in the charismatic movement. Rarely did I witness what could be described as either an inspired or credible interpretation of tongues. Interpretations were insipid, flat affirmations that God was pleased with the worship. Placed against one another, the tongues could last as long as ten minutes while the interpretation was two or three short sentences. But no one ever expressed public doubt. Having the gift was an indicator that the individual had been baptized in the Holy Ghost. Prayers for individuals to receive the gift were prevalent. I saw a young man surrounded by the elders and Smithy praying for the Holy Ghost to loosen his tongue. Each one had his arm stuck to his head. There were seven arms. After five minutes, they suddenly stopped praying and in absolute synchronicity stepped back. Smithy looked him square in the face and said, "Speak in faith." The man was dumbfounded. The

tiny circle of men around him acted as an optical lens, focusing the tension of the congregation on him. He blabbered, "Goo goo." Smithy was ecstatic, "Praise God." The man kept repeating "Goo goo." The congregation clapped. The next step was to become fluent in the language of the Holy Ghost. This meant adding a full repertoire of sounds that could be sustained over a stretch of time. I was fluent like nobody's business.

29. One of the basic tenets of the church was a concept called the blessings of Abraham in which God blessed Abraham with the fat of the land. To be saved and in the Spirit enabled one to claim these gifts. The saved individual was loaded with riches. The ruling elite inside the church professed and lived this tenet. Smithy bragged about eating steak every night. Part of Fain's cachet in the church was based on his Lincoln Continental. Men audibly dreamed of owning Cadillacs. Testimonies of money appearing in mailboxes sent from God were common. A technique to acquire the blessing of Abraham was to place a picture of the desired object on the refrigerator and every time one went by, to touch it and claim it in God's name. At the same time, images of Heaven circulating in the church resembled resort hotels with hot tubs, streets of gold, and personalized mansions based on the individual's works and faith.

30. Marx begins his chapter on commodities as a physicist dealing with the elementary units of the capitalist world. He then shifts his persona to that of an archaeologist unearthing the commodity and finding congealed labor in the heart of the labyrinth. This was a huge discovery tantamount to the discovery of Troy. But by the end of the chapter, as Marx slips and slides through the corridors of exchange value and the sticky depths of congealed labor, finding Minotaur after Minotaur grazing on bones, his persona slips again. Now he is an exorcist, and the commodity has become an utterly mysterious thing closer to Gogol's haunted overcoat wandering the streets of St. Petersburg than an elementary unit of the economy. Here Marx nudges closer to George Fluid's assessment of what possesses a commodity. Marx in his section on commodity fetishism invokes the séance table, a grotesque wooden brain threatening to jump like a monstrous insect with its wooden legs on a family at supper. "It not only stands with its feet on the

ground, but in relation to all other commodities, it stands on its head, and evolves out of its wooden brain grotesque ideas, far more wonderful than if it were to begin dancing of its own free will." Karl Marx, *Capital*, 1: 163–64.

In the analysis of my commodity infection, George begins with music. But certain representations are connected to sound in circulation, not just by music per se but rather by rock and roll specifically. The screaming face on the cover becomes a sign for the music. There is a history to this equation that leads back to the separation of race and class in the declining Jim Crow South, back to the Victorian notions of Africa as the Dark Continent. Likewise George's assessment of books is genre driven. What activates the particular genre of books or music are the bodies and their configuration inside the shape. Marx and George agree on forms of congealed labor and congealed sin at the center of a commodity.

Finally my furniture is identified. Here labor is curiously mixed up with market aura and origin. Sears purifies the commodity. It is not labor that is the source of infection or value. It is the circulation of the object and how this animates the body that is critical.

THE STARS BENEATH ALABAMA

1. On the early 1970s TV series *Night Gallery*, I saw an episode about what were called sin eaters. Food was set around the dead individual. The sin eater was brought in and he stuffed himself with the meats, breads, and sauces. As he ate, he sucked the individual's sins into his fat, leaving the dead translucent. Memory was gorging until I could feel the skin on my stomach stretch over my grandmother's gaze. This is the softer version of the architectural technology Foucault describes as the panoptic. Wrapped inside the skin gaze is the experience of sin and the hoped-for redemption. The sin isn't just a personal experience. It is a historical formation. "The sins of the fathers are visited on their sons."

2. "These arcades, a recent invention of industrial luxury, are glass-roofed, marble-paneled corridors extending through whole blocks of buildings, whose owners have joined together for such enterprises. Lining both sides of these corridors, which get their light from above, are the most elegant shops, so that

the *passage* is a city, a world in miniature." Walter Benjamin, *The Arcades Project,* trans. Howard Eiland and Kevin McLaughlin (Cambridge, Mass.: Harvard University Press, 1999), 3.

3. "Praying Mantis 'European Mantid' 2–2½ inches, including wings, which extend beyond abdominal tip, green to tan. Compound eyes tan to chocolate brown, darker at night. *Habitat:* Meadows, on foliage and flowers. *Food:* Diurnal insects, including caterpillars, flies, butterflies, bees, and some moths. This mantid was accidentally introduced in 1899 on nursery stock from southern Europe. At a time when Gypsy Moth Caterpillars were burgeoning in the eastern states, it was recognized almost immediately as a beneficial predator. However, mantids are so cannibalistic that they are rarely numerous enough to have much effect in depleting caterpillar populations." *National Audubon Society Field Guide to North American Insects and Spiders* (New York: Alfred A. Knopf, 1980), 397.

4. "The mantid Gonatista grisea, when lurking in ambush beside the lichens it imitates, is extremely easy to overlook." Thomas Eisner, *For Love of Insects* (Cambridge, Mass.: Harvard University Press, 2003), 297.

5. "The mantidae were probably the first insects on earth. This may be inferred from the fact that the Mantis protogea, whose fossil print was found in the Oeningen Myocena, belongs to the Paleodictyoptera group, which is defined by Scudder and can be traced back to the carboniferous age." Roger Caillois, *The Edge of Surrealism* (Durham, N.C.: Duke University Press, 2003), 70.

6. Walter Benjamin, "The Image of Proust," in *Selected Writings,* vol. 2, *1927–1934,* ed. Michael W. Jennings, Howard Eiland, and Gary Smith (Cambridge, Mass.: Harvard University Press, 1999), 242.

7. "And when I asked Paul Eluard about the magnificent mantis collection in his home, he confessed that he viewed their habits as the ideal mode of sexual relationship. The act of love, he said, diminishes the male and aggrandizes the female; so it is natural that she should use her ephemeral superiority to devour, or at least to kill, the male. Dalí's case is even better to use, given his paranoid-critical study of Millet's *Angelus,* which is a very complete and impressive document on

the relationship between love and cannibalism. He could hardly avoid citing the fearsome insect that actually unites these two savage desires." Roger Caillois, *The Edge of Surrealism*, 76–77.

8. "Patent-leather Beetle. Description: shiny black. Head has a short horn, forward directed. Habitat: deciduous forests. Food: adult eats decaying wood." *Audubon Society Field Guide to Insects and Spiders*, 555.

9. While Benjamin may have imagined himself as some kind of solitary wood beetle, I saw myself as a praying mantis. I identified with the insect's slenderness, folded arms, and the way its head turns contemplatively to the side scrutinizing the fly. There is a school picture of me in the second grade: crewcut, skinny, my head is cocked to the side. I'm wearing a hooded sweatshirt that in my mind made me a monastic insect knight on the run.

10. Surrounding the actors is the haze or the vapor given off from commodities. It is the collective representation of the initial mystery Marx pointed to in commodity fetishism where labor as a human endeavor disappears into the activities of things or the feel of velvet. The plush surfaces of the commodity supersede the human. Their substitution goes further than ordinarily allowed. Commodity fetishization makes possible a rethinking of the oedipal circuit in the household and tactilizes the unconscious. The tissue of the unconscious is composed of things like blue velvet cushions, hardwood floors, the cold porcelain in the bathroom, the fluff on the mother's slippers, and the constellation of objects surrounding the actors in Freud's family dream. The haze, like the white snow sweeping across the static screen of a TV in the family room, infiltrates the eye lazily slipping back into the socket.

11. Benjamin, "A Berlin Chronicle," in *Selected Writings*, vol. 2, *1927–1934*, 635.

12. "This insect really seems to be a machine with highly advanced parts, which can operate automatically. Indeed, it strikes me that likening the mantis to an automaton (to a female android, given the latter's anthropomorphism) reflects the same emotional theme, if (as I have every reason to believe) the notion of an artificial, mechanical, inanimate and unconscious machine—woman—

incommensurate with man and all living creatures—does stem in some way from a specific view of the relations between love and death and, in particular, from an ambivalent premonition of encountering one within the other." Roger Caillois, *The Edge of Surrealism*, 78–79.

13. What *The Arcades Project* lacked was the creeping luxuriant narration of "A Berlin Chronicle." The personal narrator is missing and is mechanically reproduced in the phalanx of samples like those in Benjamin's earlier surrealist text *One-Way Street*. The book exemplified the strolling, distracted eye and the montage style associated with the surrealist and the flaneur. The flaneur's mixing of public and private spaces also raises interesting questions about how autoethnographic writing can become critical and not just revelatory. The answer lies in the strategic use of the personal to make explicit the boundaries separating the public and the private and how these lines are patrolled and regulated. This means a self-conscious manipulation of one's own experiences to lure "the police" out into the open and the willingness to see how deeply hegemony has penetrated the author, making him a kind of accomplice in the very process under criticism. As for the flaneur, style is the momentary escape route and the basis of the fleeting critique. Each piece in *One-Way Street* was organized around a phrase, a common phrase lifted from a street sign like the title or "This Space for Rent" and then read as an inadvertent social commentary. Once reset, the phrase opens up suggestive lines for rereading familiar experiences. Benjamin's move also suggests how street signs, directions, and advertisements caption and frame our experiences. The direction "push" on the door points out an ambiguity around how even simple things work and hints at a combination of passivity and aggression as well as a silent authoritarianism. More than a direction, "push" is an experiential caption. What Benjamin suggests is that writing is part of a politics that extends from the page to the street. By constructing a text out of bits and fragments, Benjamin was attempting to shock the tangible into speaking. Adorno would later describe Benjamin's obsession as a kind of sorcery, at best a mystical Marxism. What holds the page in place is the implicit and overt grammar reproduced in the street signs and the shop windows. By unhinging pieces from their normal frame or position, Benjamin creates holes in the grammar. Through these holes Benjamin put together a new kind of political writing. Writing in bursts of

short episodic passages, Benjamin was attempting to build a network of interconnected fragments in which the layers in the writing would produce a heated-up reading like layers of quilts piled on a sleeping body.

14. Benjamin, "A Berlin Chronicle," 614; my emphasis.

15. Franz Kafka, "The Burrow," in *Franz Kafka: The Complete Stories* (New York: Schocken Books, 1971), 235; my emphasis.

16. Diana Fuss, *The Sense of an Interior: Four Writers and the Rooms That Shaped Them* (New York: Routledge, 2004), 163; my emphasis.

17. "If once we were able to view the Borges tale in which the cartographers of the Empire draw up a map so detailed that it ends up covering the territory exactly (the decline of the Empire witnesses the fraying of this map, little by little, and its fall into ruins, though some shreds are still discernible in the deserts—the metaphysical beauty of this ruined abstraction testifying to a pride equal to the Empire and rotting like a carcass, returning to the substance of the soil, a bit as the double ends by being confused with the real through aging) . . ." Jean Baudrillard, *Simulacra and Simulation,* trans. Sheila Faria Glaser (Ann Arbor: University of Michigan Press, 1994), 1.

18. "Leaning over in his hammock, Queequeg long regarded the coffin with an attentive eye. He then called for his harpoon, had the wooden stock drawn from it, and then had the iron part placed in the coffin along with one of the paddles of his boat. All by his own request, also, biscuits were then ranged round the sides within: a flask of freshwater was placed at the head, and a small bag of woody earth scraped up in the hold at the foot; and a piece of sailcloth being rolled up for a pillow, Queequeg now entreated to be lifted into his final bed, that he might make trial of its comforts, if any it had. He lay without moving a few minutes, then told one to go to his bag and bring out his little god, Yojo. Then crossing his arms on his breast with Yojo between, he called for the coffin lid . . . to be placed over him. The head part turned over with a leather hinge, and there lay Queequeg in his coffin with little but his composed countenance in view." Herman Melville, *Moby-Dick, or The Whale* (New York: Penguin Books, 2001), 522.

19. AC and I had driven across Pelham and down a deeply shaded side street. There is a Waffle House on the corner there laid out singularly in the bright sun. The drive was short. We pulled up next to an old brick house. There was an out-side staircase to the second floor. The stairway was clogged with garbage. Underneath that I could feel something akin to my grandmother's house—the same wood, a similar smell, the color and size of the banister strung like a black boa constrictor the length of the stairs. My grandfather was in a black suit. He had his walking stick, what he called his farm stick. The house had been rented to college students who had skipped out without paying the rent. The house was grand. It must have been gorgeous in the late 1800s and in the early twentieth century. It would have looked at World War I with a beautiful stare beneath the magnolias. Now the house was like a luxury steamship abandoned in the Amazon jungle or a victim of a weird strategic bombing that ate its insides and left its exterior intact. My grandfather sold it. Its rental value was emptied. The house was leveled. And what parts that could have been Amazonian were buried in a landfill at the edge of Crooked Mountain Road. The tree canopy cut away, the extravagance and luxury were decimated in a flash. He did not grieve its passing.

20. "So, floating on the margin of the ensuing scene, and in full sight of it, when the half-spent suction of the sunk ship reached me, I was then, but slowly, drawn towards the closing vortex. When I reached it, it had subsided to a creamy pool. Round and round, and then, and ever contracting towards the button-like black bubble at the axis of that slowly wheeling circle, like another Ixion I did revolve. Till, gaining that vital centre, the black bubble upward burst; and now, liberated by reason of its cunning spring, and owing to its great buoyancy, rising with great force, the coffin life-buoy shot lengthwise from the sea, fell over, and floated by my side. Buoyed up by that coffin, for almost one whole day and night, I floated on a soft and dirge-like main. The unharming sharks, they glided by as if with padlocks on their mouths; the savage seahawks sailed with sheathed beaks. On the second day, a sail drew near, nearer, and picked me up at last." Melville, *Moby-Dick*, 625.

21. Michael Taussig tells a story about a vendor in the market in Bogotá, Colombia. Around this tale he has fashioned the frame of the rubber boom in Colombia

in the first years of the twentieth century. At the time, so many Indians were slaughtered that their bodies were figured into the weight of the rubber. This much fat per pound of rubber. "The crowd is thick and milling there on Twenty-sixth Street, the day of the lost souls of Purgatory. The crowd is swarming like bees. What is going on? On top of a step ladder is perched a square wooden box, each side about 3 feet long. For 100 pesos the man on the street with a mega-phone will open the doors of the box. Inside, expressionless, is a bodiless boy. Sweet—sweet as an angel. In his mouth he holds the corner of an airmail letter. It contains a prophecy. It's yours for 100 pesos. The doors close on the bodiless face. We want to see more. So sweet. Doors to the future revealed by the cut-off child." I can't get over the letter. I wonder if its stamp is an icon, a thumbprint in color stuck on the corner, a saint standing in orchids, or a Jaguar stretched out on a limb mimicking the State, another kind of magic hiding in the foliage. The letter goes unopened. Taussig doesn't have to open it to understand what would be written. The Anglo-Saxon words are irrelevant. The important point is that the letter is a body double for the Indian boy displayed like a rich chocolate in a box. The magic is in the inscription across the body—the letter is a portable sign for the 32,000 Indians killed during the boom, the Indian shamans macheted by whites in the countryside, and the Indian-powered healing curios, which all fit hand in glove—body and violence together—and to what Taussig describes as a "culture of terror." Michael Taussig, *Shamanism, Colonialism, and the Wild Man* (Chicago: University of Chicago Press, 1987), 186.

22. "Combs swim about, frog-green and coral-red, as in an aquarium; trumpets turn to conches, ocarinas to umbrella handles; and lying in the fixative pans from a photographer's darkroom is birdseed." Benjamin, *The Arcades Project,* 872.

23. Karl Marx, *Capital* (New York: Vintage Books, 1977), 1:125; my emphasis.

24. William Wood, nine years old, was seven years ten months old when he began to work. He "ran moulds" (carried ready-molded articles into the dry-ing room, afterward bringing back the empty mold) from the very beginning. He came to work every day in the week at 6 a.m. and left off at about 9 p.m. "I work

till 9 o'clock at night six days in the week. I have done so for the last seven or eight weeks." Marx, *Capital*, 1:354.

25. Marx, *Capital*, 1: 940; my emphasis.

26. Ibid., 1: 163; my emphasis.

27. Ibid., 1: 364.

28. Ibid., 1: 847.

29. Georges Perec, *Life: A User's Manual*, trans. David Bellos (Boston: David R. Godine, 1987), 123.

30. Jean-Paul Sartre, *Being and Nothingness* (New York: Philosophical Library, 1956), 607–8; my emphasis.

31. The newer translation renders "iron cage" into "steel coating," which by most accounts is closer to what Weber intended. With the steel coating translation, Weber's concept of character itself becoming an enclosure is clearer as is the closeness and completeness of the fit, literally a steel skin. But the image of iron has certain valuable connotations. The first is its weight pressing on the person, even from a distance, with a magnetic force field. The second is its echo of Marx's opening equation in *Capital* in which twenty pounds of linen equal one coat is eventually transmuted into iron. Here we have the crushing weight Weber was reaching for facing the everydayness across an equals sign. And then there are the physical characteristics of iron: it rusts, it smells, it is brittle at certain temperatures, and it is able to hold heat longer—a vestigial humanness persists even if the human goes out. Max Weber, *The Protestant Ethic and the Spirit of Capitalism*, trans. Talcott Parsons (New York: Charles Scribner's Sons, 1958), 181.

32. Marcel Proust, *Swann's Way*, trans. Lydia Davis (London: Penguin Books, 2002), 47–48; my emphasis.

33. Walter Benjamin, *One-Way Street*, in *Selected Writings*, vol. 1, *1913–1926*, 444.

34. Franz Kafka, "The Burrow," 346–47; my emphasis.

35. Franz Kafka, *America (The Man Who Disappeared),* trans. Michael Hofmann (New York: New Directions, 2002), 29–30.

ASSEMBLING MARY PULLEN FOR A CRY

1. Michel Foucault, *Discipline and Punish: The Birth of the Prison,* trans. Alan Sheridan (New York: Vintage, 1979), 5–6.

2. Ibid.

3. Walter Benjamin, *One-Way Street,* in *Selected Writings,* vol. 1, *1913–1926,* ed. Michael Bullock and Michael W. Jennings (Cambridge, Mass.: Harvard University Press, 1996), 445.

4. Gilles Deleuze and Félix Guattari, *Anti-Oedipus: Capitalism and Schizophrenia,* trans. Robert Hurley et al. (Minneapolis: University of Minnesota Press, 1983).

5. Raymond Williams, *Marxism and Literature* (Oxford: Oxford University Press, 1977).

6. Pierre Bourdieu, *The Logic of Practice,* trans. Richard Nice (Stanford, Calif.: Stanford University Press, 1990).

7. Benjamin, "A Berlin Chronicle," in *Selected Writings,* vol. 2, *1927–1934,* 611.

8. Foucault, *Discipline and Punish,* 293.

9. Walter Benjamin, *A Berlin Childhood around 1900,* trans. Howard Eiland (New Haven, Conn.: Harvard University Press, 2006), 134.

10. Charles Darwin, *The Origin of Species* (New York: Penguin Books, 1985), 459.

Illustrations

Publication History

Portions of an early version of "The Mark on the Spade" were previously published as "The Mineralization of John Pelham," *Ecopoetics* 3 (Winter 2003).

An earlier version of "The Mark on the Spade" was published by Sage Publications in *Cultural Studies and Critical Methodologies* 3, no. 3 (August 2003): 287–307.

An earlier version of "Planchette, My Love" was published by Sage Publications in *Cultural Studies and Critical Methodologies* 6, no. 3 (August 2006): 311–29.

Portions of an early version of "Planchette, My Love" were published as "The Devil inside Me," *Radical Society* 30, no. 3–4 (2004): 29–37.

An early version of "The Stars beneath Alabama" appeared in *Journal of Historical Sociology* 19, no. 4 (December 2006): 474–503.

ALLEN SHELTON is associate professor of sociology at Buffalo State College in Buffalo, New York. He worked previously on A. C. Shelton's Angus Farm and with Arthur Rollin's carpentry crew before taking an appointment as a lecturer at Auburn University in 1988. Since then he has traveled the country as an academic.